I0022107

Quarterly Essay

CONTENTS

Quarterly Essay is published four times a year by Black Inc., an imprint of Schwartz Publishing Pty Ltd
Publisher: Morry Schwartz

ISBN 186 395 1970

Subscriptions (4 issues): $49 a year within Australia incl. GST (Institutional subs. $59). Outside Australia $79. Payment may be made by Mastercard, Visa or Bankcard, or by cheque made out to Schwartz Publishing. Payment includes postage and handling.

To subscribe, fill out and post the subscription form on the last page of this essay, or subscribe online at:

www.quarterlyessay.com

Correspondence and subscriptions should be addressed to the Editor at:
Black Inc.
Level 5, 289 Flinders Lane
Melbourne VIC 3000 Australia
Phone: 61 3 9654 2000
Fax: 61 3 9654 2290
Email: quarterlyessay@blackincbooks.com
http://www.quarterlyessay.com

Editor: Chris Feik
Management: Sophy Williams
Editorial Co-ordinator: Caitlin Yates
Publicity: Meredith Kelly
Design: Guy Mirabella

LATHAM'S WORLD

The New Politics of the Outsiders

Margaret Simons

Spotlight renders even soft things sharp. The faces of primary-school children can cast dark shadows.

It was mid-June and what could have been a cheerless night, but we were at the Melbourne Concert Hall watching children from the schools of the western suburbs perform. There were dances and clowns and singing and mini-orchestras. We parents pretended not to cry, not to be moved by youth and hope and our own role in making the future.

Then a primary-school choir from Altona took the stage, and their act dried our tears and wiped our smiles. The children were dressed in black and white. They didn't smile. They sang that anthem of the ignored, "What About Me?" They sang with conviction. They belted it out.

What about me? It isn't fair
I've had enough, now I want my share,
Can't you see, I wanna live
But you just take more

You just take more
You just take more than you give
What about me? ...
What about me? ...
What about me? ...

They placed their hands over their hearts as they sang the last three lines. The music stopped. The spotlight dimmed.

"I've always hated that song," said one of the middle-class mums at the interval. Our school's children had sung the entirely unthreatening "Turn the Lights On". They had been acceptably optimistic.

Once the western suburbs meant disadvantage. That is one of the reasons why the Westside Concert is held – to build self-esteem and cultural capital. But things have changed in the inner west. Most of the children on stage, including my own, were from the arc of comfort within sight of the city towers. The Altona kids were an exception. Altona is an industrial suburb on the frayed edges of the city. It plots its history through the industries established there – petrochemical plants, salt works – and the slow, slow stretch of basic services from the centre to the fringe. So close to the winter solstice and the turning point of the year, and within months of the federal election, the kids from Altona had put us on notice. The fringe is no longer content to serve the centre. In politics, the fringe obligates and defines us all.

This is an essay about the alternative prime minister, Mark Latham. It is not biography, although with this politician more than most the life story is part of the political. There will be plenty of Latham biographies. Some of them will have been published before you read this. I am more interested in what the Latham phenomenon means than in the man himself, although the two things are inevitably linked. Personality is about values, and values are, or should be, about policy. Certainly with Latham they are. He is a conviction politician. Even his political opponents acknowledge this, and the most superficial examination of his life and his books confirms it. He is ambitious, but not an opportunist. His passion makes him frightening, as well as exciting.

Newspaper clippings from his first forays into public life have him describing himself as a "club buster". More recently, and more acceptably, he has said that Labor needs to define itself as an anti-establishment party, "Australia's natural party of outsiders". He has always believed, and wanted others to believe, that politics has the power to change lives, in particular the lives of children like those from the Altona primary schools.

I think it is clear that if Labor gains power there will be fundamental changes to Australia – the biggest Latham can manage. They will include changes to our understanding of what it is to be poor and what it is to be privileged, and of what equality might entail.

Mark Latham has written that all of us need to embrace multiple identities. We are members of families, members of ethnic groups, supporters of our sporting teams, and also Australians. Our allegiances shift, contract and expand. I know what he means. When I turn my mind to national politics, I see it from at least two perspectives. On the one hand, I am on the inside. I am a journalist and a writer. I interview politicians. Things I have written might even have been influential, in a tiny way. I number among my friends some of the powerful. In this role I am engaged with, even fascinated by, the spectator sport of politics.

At the same time I am a parent. I stand in the schoolyard with other parents, and we talk. I cannot avoid the alienation, the disconnection and the cynicism of those around me. I feel some of it myself. Most people don't like politics. Perhaps this is why it has to be coated in faux scandal – to make it palatable, and to persuade us that the work of the Canberra press gallery is important and relevant. Then again, alienation from public life must in part be because it is reported in such an unappealing way – alternately boring and salacious.

On the night of the Westside Concert we parents were meant to be in the grip of election fever according to the commentators, many of whom were confidently predicting an August election. Resigned to the descent of the campaign might have been more accurate for most of us. When we are together, we parents don't talk politics, or not in the sense of discussing policies or politicians. In another sense we talk about nothing else. We talk about classroom sizes, and child-care, and working and raising kids, and traffic flows through our suburbs, and the choice between private and public education. Mention the election or a politician, and the conversation tends to die. I think most of the parents no longer believe that politicians make a difference to the things that touch their lives. There seem to be no ideas, no narrative, to engage us or to harness the small practicalities of the schoolyard and the neighbourhood to some sense of national direction. I think Mark Latham might change this, if he can make himself heard, and this is one of the things I like about him. One thing links my identities. Always, I badly *want* politics to matter.

At a dinner party recently, I halted a political argument by reading aloud the first few pages of Latham's most recent book, *From the Suburbs*. The silence afterwards lasted for minutes. It was both alarmed and impressed. "There are more ideas there", said one of the people present, "than I have heard in politics for years."

The way politics is reported will surely be as big a barrier to Latham's election as anything John Howard might or might not do. It is difficult, in Australia at present, to communicate an idea. Even when someone succeeds, ideas in politics are treated with suspicion. They are dangerous — indications that the present state of things may not be sustained. Those in the comfort zone, which includes most journalists and others in the political classes, will always resist true change, while those who are less secure will likely be more susceptible to the radical.

Mark Latham makes me nervous. In my writing and journalistic life, my friends and I are among those who have grown a carapace, multiple chips on the shoulder and habits of caution from being denigrated as "chattering classes" and the "elite". During the Howard years this denigration has robbed us of some of our undoubted comfort, but we have had the ultimate consolation: the sense of our own righteousness. I think Mark Latham is unlikely to leave that sense intact.

His vision is materialistic, but not only materialistic. He says the big divisions in politics are no longer those of capital and labour, or even of income. Rather, they are cultural, and to do with power. There are insiders and outsiders. The insiders are people like me, and probably the majority of readers of this essay. We are the information-rich, those adept in navigating the information age, and who therefore feel relatively secure in a fast-changing world. Latham includes in this class both the left-wing "chattering classes" derided during the Howard years, and also the elites of the right – newspaper commentators, those elevated to the key cultural posts of the nation and the leaders of big business.

The outsiders, on the other hand, are those who do not feel confident or knowledgeable about anything other than the immediate things of their lives – services, schools, the micro-changes of politics. The outsiders live on the fringes of cities, and in the regions. If the insiders, in the words of the Altona choir, "take more than they give", it is not in money, or not only in money. It is in their hoarding of political and cultural power.

Latham has written:

> I would argue that the political spectrum is best understood as a struggle between insiders and outsiders – the abstract values of the powerful centre, versus the pragmatic beliefs of those who feel disenfranchised by social change. This is a different framework to class-based politics. Rather than drawing their identity from the economic system, people see their place in society as a reflection of their access to information and public influence. The insiders/outsiders divide has become a reliable guide to electoral behaviour.

The divide explains the rise of Pauline Hanson, Latham says. It explains why Australians voted down a republic with a politician-appointed president, even though most wanted an Australian head of state. It explains the failure of Paul Keating, and the success of John Howard. If Latham succeeds, it will explain his victory.

Mark Latham's ideas for change are not chiefly about the economy. He has described the reforms introduced by Hawke and Keating – opening the Australian economy to the world, floating the dollar – as Part One of a program that has now stalled. Part Two should be to do with society itself. He has written, in contradiction of Mrs Thatcher's famous pronouncement, that "there is such a thing as society." Latham's ideas concern how we relate to each other, our mutual obligations and our values. He sees himself as the leader of Part Two.

Latham's roots lie not in the Hawke and Keating years but in an earlier phase of Australian Labor Party history. In both a literal and a broader sense, he is Gough Whitlam's heir – the successor to Whitlam's seat of Werriwa in Sydney's outer west and the first political leader since Whitlam to talk mainly about society, rather than economics. Latham spent his early years of adulthood deeply engaged both with Gough Whitlam the man and with the legacy of the Whitlam government. He does not share the conventional view of Whitlam as flawed visionary who tried to do too much too soon and was brought down by poor economic management.

On the day of the Westside Concert, I read an interview with the author Shirley Hazzard, who had just won the Miles Franklin Award for her novel *The Great Fire*. The article described her as "coiffed, frail, a speaker in sculpted, thoughtful sentences". Hazzard still wrote on a type-writer. She represented a genteel past, and also the time when a literary life, an intellectual life, was just beginning to be a possibility in Australia – although Hazzard, like so many others, felt she had to leave. Hazzard commented on modern times:

> Language is being diminished. Politicians are out of touch. We are living in a world that wants attestable things, when the inattestable things are what has made life more liveable. The poetic side of life. Introspection. Mysterious things. Humility.

I think it is manifest that Hazzard's view is one with which Mark Latham would be radically out of sympathy. I suspect Hazzard is right, and we live in an age of attestable things — of analytical thought, but not abstract thought. Of outsider thinking, rather than the examined life of the insiders. If Latham becomes prime minister, that thinking will become even more dominant in Australia. It will come into its own politically.

I am with Hazzard on the inattestable things. Yet at the same time, I can sniff the cold wind of change and it excites me. Reading about Hazzard's typewriter, I roll my eyes. Part of me wants to pummel her sculpted sentences. I believe that people like me need a change, a shock and a challenge. And we know, don't we, after the events of the last few years, that we are out of touch? That somehow our country has slipped beyond our understanding and our influence?

Even if Latham fails, the country will still be altered. Part of this is "generational change", but I think that phrase is being used too glibly, without thought for what it means. A change of generations is not only about age, but also about life experience — the times we have lived through.

Mark Latham is forty-three years old, a year younger than me. We are part of the tag end of the baby-boomer generation — almost not baby boomers at all, yet not young enough to be part of Generation X. Like me, Latham was a teenager when Gough Whitlam was dismissed. He is too young to have been part of the great social upheavals of the '60s, too young to have been called up or at risk of call-up for Vietnam, too young to have been a hippie. Yet he and I are old enough to have been formed by the aftermath of these events and social changes, both good and bad. I think people our age combine a sense of pragmatism, edging into disappointment, with a sense of big possibility. We are old enough to know that economics was not always the only thing in political life — that once society mattered too. That once there were big ideas.

If Latham ascends to power, then it will be signal of succession to our generation. We will be in our prime. It will be our turn to run the place, and I am sure things will be different.

"What's his *story*?" I asked Michael Byrne, one of Latham's oldest friends. I wanted to know how Latham saw himself – what narratives he had to give his life meaning. What sense he had of a world beyond the pragmatic – how he understood the nature of things. Byrne is a devout Catholic of the socially reforming kind. He and Latham used to eat together at an Indian restaurant in Liverpool. Latham would always take the corner seat, next to the window, so he could watch "his voters" walking by.

Once Byrne and Latham were knocking a golf ball around on a course at the edge of the city. It was a blokey friendship. They talked politics endlessly, but rarely delved into personal matters. On this occasion there was greater intimacy. Byrne talked a bit about Jesus Christ. Latham was interested, but not because of any spiritual inclination. Rather he was interested in the politics. How had Christ managed to found a movement that survived so long after his death? How had the ideas been communicated? Byrne suggested that divinity might have had something to do with it. He knew as he said the words that Latham would not only disagree, but would not really understand the concept.

Michael Byrne suggested to me that the Labor Party was Latham's "story", but I don't think that can be true. Latham has been fighting the party for most of his life. One of the notable things about him is that his success has been achieved largely in spite of the Labor Party machine, and without significant support from any of its factions. His support base has been built from outside the party. Unlike most of the leaders who preceded him, he owes very few favours.

Would we have poetry, I asked Michael Byrne? Would Latham do that thing that leaders do – that Keating had done – spin us a yarn, tell us a story, tell us what it all means, and where we might be going?

The answer is no. Mark Latham's vision is a series of small pictures, rather than the big picture of Paul Keating.

"You won't get poetry from him," Byrne replied. "But he's the kind of man who'll keep a poet around him."

Gough Whitlam is eighty-eight, and old in every sense of the word. He has never been a particularly easy interview subject. These days it is difficult to gain an audience at all, let alone keep him on topic. He rings Mark Latham's office frequently, I am told, with snippets of advice and reassurance. In the Labor Party everyone knows that Gough loves Mark, and that the love is returned. Whitlam has been promoting Latham for years, telling all those who still listen to him that the party's fortunes would be revived only when Mark Latham was leader. So far as Whitlam is concerned, Latham is his anointed heir. "If Mark becomes prime minister, I think Gough will die soon after," one friend told me. "He will see his life's work as being complete."

Whitlam talked to me on the telephone for nearly an hour, but it was difficult to keep him on track. He wanted to talk about the history of the Balkans, and he gave me a hard time for not being completely up on the topic. There were plenty of flashes of wit. "I am a has-been, but I'm a bloody good has-been," he intoned.

He recounted how he had met Latham, and how Latham had impressed him. He was keen to emphasise one thing. He objected to people calling him Latham's mentor. "I am not his mentor. I am his tutor." Later I asked him what the difference was, and the answer came back communicated through his secretary. "A mentor is one who advises. A tutor is one who teaches." But words carry a freight of history.

Mentor was Ulysses' friend. When Ulysses embarked on his epic journey, he appointed Mentor as counsellor for the family he left behind, in particular his son Telemachus. The word "tutor", on the other hand, comes to the English language through French and Latin. Its original meaning had little to do with teaching. It meant guardian or protector. This is the kind of thing that Gough Whitlam would almost certainly know.

Mark Latham's father Don did not appoint Gough Whitlam as Ulysses did Telemachus. When Latham and Whitlam first encountered each other, it was guardianship rather than mentorship that Latham needed. That, and a reason to hope.

Don Latham has acquired a patina over the last few months; he has been posthumously reconstructed. One suspects that the greatest significance lies in the things that are not said about him. Latham has a little mantra about his father which he has delivered on several occasions. It goes like this: Don Latham was loving and caring, proud of his son's achievements, but also a gambler whose habit – "a sickness" – kept the family poor. Latham's sister has said that Don was not only a gambler, but also a drinker. Mark Latham says the drinking was never a problem. Don Latham is remembered by his mates as quiet, proud of his family, ordinary. Many never dreamt he had a gambling problem. He was not the dominant force in the household. That was Latham's mother, a strong and protective woman who kept the family together. Latham has said that he wears the tag "Mummy's boy" with pride. The bond between mother and son was so strong that those who knew Latham and his first wife could sense the tension between the two women. "Did you get to know Latham's mother?" I asked one of Latham's close friends from his days on Liverpool Council. "No. She was only interested in knowing Mark."

Don Latham died when Mark was just nineteen and starting his university career. His death precipitated a double crisis in Latham's life. His studies were at risk, and his mother chose this time to reveal the truth about Don's gambling, which had until then been a secret. The crisis in Latham's education was overcome, with help, about which more later.

The greater crisis seems to have been resolved by Whitlam, who became, in the words of Latham's mother, "like a second father". When Latham finished university, Whitlam hired him as his secretary and researcher. Together they worked on the big book The Whitlam Government 1972–1975, which was Whitlam's attempt to set the historical record straight.

Whitlam's son, Nick Whitlam, remembers the young Mark Latham being introduced to the family in the early 1980s and rapidly becoming "the honorary fifth child". Whitlam was a hard taskmaster and Latham was "the one who passed all the tests". Nick Whitlam bears no malice or jealousy. He likes Mark Latham. Whitlam had complete faith in him.

What drew the two men together? What attracted Gough? It seems to have been a combination of Latham's sharp mind and his knockabout, rough-edged background.

Whitlam had a breadth of intellect but was sheltered in the way that those of us born to comfort and education must always be sheltered. Latham had an intellect to match but also a larrikin side. Gabrielle Gwyther, Latham's former wife, says that the two men taught each other a lot. Whitlam educated Latham about history and culture, and about the record of his government. Latham took his "tutor" around the seamier parts of Paris.

Both men were at turning points in their life when they met. Whitlam had just left politics. The book he was working on with Latham was, Nick Whitlam remembers, extraordinarily important to him. He wanted to make sure that his legacy was remembered accurately. When Whitlam was appointed Ambassador to UNESCO by the Hawke government, he took Latham to Paris with him. For Latham, Whitlam's patronage must have been the first time the world had given him a clear sign that his brains, wit and ambition were not doomed to wither in obscurity. Nothing else in his life, apart from academic achievement and his mother's love, would have given him so much reason to hope.

Mark Latham was brought up in Green Valley, near Liverpool and in Whitlam's seat of Werriwa on the south-western fringe of Sydney. Green Valley was a Housing Commission settlement created by a state government pursuing ideas and ideals with little heed for the effect they had on people's lives. Public-housing tenants from the inner city were moved to a dust bowl far from any services: the roads were clay, the telephone was miles away at the local store, it was a five-kilometre walk to the railway station, and there were no buses. Today the houses of Green Valley remain, some clad in plastic faux-brick, with the occasional two-storey extension testifying to more wealth and aspiration than existed in the 1960s.

There is a passage about Green Valley in Whitlam's book. One fancies Mark Latham might have had a hand in it:

> Green Valley became a cultural and recreational wasteland, permeated
> by an appallingly high incidence of vandalism, juvenile delinquency,
> petty crime and family breakdown. Hugh Stretton described the area
> as "among this century's most deliberate, unnecessary, concentrated
> and massive offences against Australia's children".

It was Green Valley that Whitlam cited as the inspiration for one of the enduring features of his government: its focus on the quality of life in cities. For both men, Liverpool and its surrounds was an enduring inspiration and a spur to action. But for Latham it was also his home.

Gabrielle Gwyther says that it was Whitlam who taught Mark Latham how to write, and how to use political language. Nick Whitlam concurs. He points out that Whitlam and Latham are unusual among Labor leaders in having an Anglo-Saxon, rather than an Anglo-Celtic background.

Keating had a touch of the Irish blarney. One could sense in his agenda, his speeches and his persona the Irish talents for melancholia, mystery, narrative and symbol, as well as the history of resentment against colonial powers, particularly the English.

Whitlam and Latham, on the other hand, use a language shorn of abstracts. It is matter-of-fact, yet has a kind of thrilling simplicity. It is the kind of language that survives.

I came to political awareness with Gough's call to action – "Men and Women of Australia" – ringing in my ears. Later there was the sinewy – and futile – defiance of "Well may we say 'God Save the Queen', because nothing can save the Governor-General." Even the injunction to "Maintain your rage" survives in the public consciousness and the popular lexicon long after it has been honoured in the breach.

In more recent times it has been Latham who, even in backbench obscurity, has coined the definitive phrases of politics. Many don't realise that it was Latham, not John Howard, who coined the term "aspirational voters".

Latham's first press conference on being elected Labor leader showed two things: first, that no matter how surprised everyone else was, he had clearly been preparing for this moment. Secondly, that he understood how to use language. It was the "cut through" factor that Crean had lacked. The plain statements of purpose, the assertions both of self and of political agenda:

> I believe in ambition and aspiration. I believe in the powerful combination of hard work, good family and the civilising role of government services. I say that economic aspiration is good and social mobility is even better − all Australians climbing the ladder of opportunity.

It is a concrete language, sparing yet powerful in its use of metaphors. One cannot imagine Latham speaking, as Keating did, of "true believers". Latham's books − many of them based on his speeches − use the same kind of prose. (The exception is his magnum opus, *Civilising Global Capital*, which is, as his friend and ally Julia Gillard put it, "a book in search of an editor".)

Latham differs from Whitlam in his use of vernacular and crudity. I can't imagine Whitlam getting away with a phrase like "fair dinkum". Nor can I imagine him intoning about a "conga-line of suckholes" or "arselickers". On the other hand, it is not hard to imagine Whitlam, if he were in his prime today, describing George W. Bush as "the most dangerous and incompetent American president in living memory".

Latham's use of vernacular has been his unique contribution to Australian political speech. Cabinet minister Tony Abbott described the "arselicker" comment as vulgar and vile. Latham defended it as "a great Australian phrase, a phrase that's used throughout the nation every day, a great and accurate description of the PM's behaviour in Washington". Now Latham has promised "no more crudity", but the colloquialisms remain part of his political identity. Keating's sense of narrative and his abiding melancholy were a siren call to the educated middle class. To the aspirational voters, Latham's language must sound like a guarantee he will not get above himself.

It is ironic that Whitlam is remembered as a great visionary. During the lead-up to his taking power, he was mocked as the exact opposite. Like Latham, he was ridiculed for talking "small" and "soft" rather than about the big issues of federal government. When Whitlam talked about the nature of life in the cities, and the need to upgrade the sewerage system in outer suburbs, the Liberal Prime Minister, John Gorton, derided him as "wanting to be prime minister in the way one is shire president".

Like Latham, Whitlam was attacked for betraying key Labor values. He rejected socialism and embraced the free market. The main job of government, he said, was to work out how best to use the wealth of the country. Latham has used almost exactly the same words.

In his first book, *Reviving Labor's Agenda*, Latham made reference to Whitlam in defining the ALP as a "practical party with policies framed to meet the particular challenges of inequality". Since Whitlam, Latham wrote, inequality had not been about levels of income so much as access to community services such as education, health and transport. He quoted from *The Whitlam Government 1972–1975*:

> This concept does not have as its primary goal equality of personal income. Its goal is greater equality of the services which the community provides ... The approach is based on this concept: increasing a citizen's real standard of living, the health of himself and his family, his children's opportunity for education and self-improvement, his access to employment opportunities, his ability to enjoy the nation's resources for recreation and cultural activity,

his legacy from the national heritage, his scope to participate in the decisions and actions of the community, [these things] are determined not so much by his income as by the availability and accessibility of the services which the community alone can provide and ensure.

Some see echoes of Whitlam in Latham's handling of foreign policy – surely in most respects one of his weakest areas. In Whitlam's time, too, the alliance with the United States was under stress, so much so that for a generation conspiracy theories circulated about the CIA's role in the Prime Minister's downfall. Whitlam brought the troops home from an unpopular foreign war. Latham has (off and on) promised to bring them home from Iraq.

What links Latham with his tutor, though, is not specific policy, but rather mutual areas of concern and a similar understanding of the role of government, in particular the role of the Labor Party. Both men, in their books, have rejected socialism and centralisation of state power. Both have declared that the main concern of government is deciding how to use the country's wealth, and that this is the dividing line between Liberal and Labor politics. Both want a greater federal role in health and education. Both are interested in local government, and a redefinition of federalism. Both speak of dispersing power.

Nick Whitlam says that Mark Latham knows more about the record of the Whitlam government than any living person other than Gough himself. From doing the research on "the big book", he knows almost day by day what the Whitlam government did and tried to do – both its strengths and its mistakes. "I often think", says Nick Whitlam, "that Howard is wrong when he accuses Mark of having no experience of government. There is a sense in which he knows about government very well indeed. And he knows that there were those in the old establishment who never really acknowledged that Gough Whitlam, with his radical ideas, was entitled to be prime minister."

Julia Gillard, Shadow Minister for Health and one of Latham's inner circle, insists the world has changed too much for Latham to be "the modern iteration of Gough". Solutions that were tenable in the 1970s – such as free tertiary education – are no longer possible. She says, too, "I think he's a very different person due to background, and by dint of interests. You would probably sit down and hear Gough talk about art and music and opera, and I don't think you'd likely find Mark Latham doing that. Partly that's background and age difference. He's more likely to be talking about Meatloaf than opera, but then I'm a bit like that and I think it's just the generation we're from. The older generation were more civilised, or something like that."

Mark Latham has paid tribute to his tutor many times during his political career. In 1985, the local Liverpool newspaper published an interview with Latham, then secretary to the local ALP branch, to mark the imminent publication of Whitlam's book. Latham referred to Whitlam as "the great man" throughout, and used the opportunity to criticise the then Prime Minister, Bob Hawke:

> Whitlam had one priceless quality in politics – to put new ideas on the deck, something the present bloke doesn't have … I've learnt from Whitlam that unless you are prepared to take the initiative and lead the debate and sell your ideas to the public, the chances of getting through reform are next to nothing. You can't say Bill Hayden ever campaigned hard on an issue, or that Hawke has got ideas that he constantly tries to sell to people. They just seem to float along.

When, nine years later, Latham was elected as the member for Whitlam's old seat of Werriwa, one of the first things he did in parliament was to put eight questions on the notice paper to the Minister for Foreign Affairs, Gareth Evans, about an old hobby horse of Whitlam's – the British Museum's refusal to return the Elgin Marbles to Greece. When Latham's youngest son was born some years later, he was named Isaac Gough.

On 2 December 2003, when Latham was on his way into parliament for the vote that made him leader of the opposition, he described the date as a special one, because on that day in 1972 Whitlam had ended twenty-three years of Coalition government.

Weeks later, Latham made his first overseas trip as opposition leader to Papua New Guinea. The choice of destination was hardly a populist move – it was unlikely to swing the votes of many aspirationals. Instead it amounted to a tribute to Whitlam, who counted PNG's independence as one of his main achievements in government. It was Gough who organised the trip, by making a personal call to the PNG Prime Minister, Michael Somare.

If Latham's roots are in Whitlam, then his branches are in the Third Way – the trend in social-democratic thinking behind both Bill Clinton's and Tony Blair's ascents to power. The central idea of the Third Way is that the "old politics" of labour against capital is no longer relevant in the Information Age, and that a Third Way is needed: a synthesis of left-wing and right-wing ideology. The Third Way's unifying themes are support for a market economy as the creator of wealth and for government to act as a civiliser of the markets and a guardian and promoter of civic society and the public good.

Latham is heavily influenced by Clinton's adviser, Dick Morris, who coined the ugly word "triangulation" – the notion that left and right are extremes on a flat plane, with the Third Way sitting both between and above them, like the apex of a triangle. Latham believes in cutting through ideology to arrive at fresh, pragmatic solutions. One of the recurring phrases in his books is: "it is time to rethink things from first principles."

There are a few central ideas in Latham's books from which all else follows. As already discussed, the first is his view that the main political divide is between insiders and outsiders.

The second is a *spatial* sense of politics – the observation that privilege and poverty can increasingly be predicted by postcode, and that the main differences between Australians are not state-based, but regional. Similar regions can be found within different states: Fitzroy has more in common with Balmain than it does with Dandenong. This spatial sense leads Latham to question, and seek to redefine, Australia's federalism. In the main areas of public policy, he sees federal government as a funder, standard-setter and regulator, with service delivery being carried out by regional authorities. One of the main problems of the Left, he says, is that it has supported "bigness" in the public sector, while criticising it in the private. The Left has been against McDonalds, but for Centrelink. He wants to rethink most of the important areas of public policy from a geographic point of view. He talks about the management of *place*, which can sometimes mean a whole neighbourhood, sometimes a single public-housing estate. He wants to manage big issues in a lot of small ways.

Bedded within this local sensibility are notions about what makes a good neighbourhood: civic engagement on a micro level, mutual responsibility, and welfare, education and health systems tailored to individual circumstances and designed to bring about change. In Latham's world, for every right and entitlement there is a corresponding responsibility. It is no accident that one of those most notably influenced by Mark Latham's books has been Noel Pearson, the Aboriginal leader who is applying ideas about place and welfare to Cape York's most remote communities. Pearson has credited Latham as the main inspiration for his work.

The last, and probably the most important, of Latham's key themes is education – the topic on which he has written most, on which his ideas are most developed, and which he sees as the answer to most social ills, a public investment and a government responsibility like no other, and the main means of achieving both national prosperity and social equality and mobility.

The Third Way can mean different things to different people. The phrase has come to be regarded with such cynicism that it is in danger of losing its original meaning. Latham himself has stopped using the term, though only a few years ago he wrote that the Third Way was:

a guiding ideology, a single philosophy which links all parts of its policy program ... the true social democratic principle of our time is the dispersal of economic, social and political power ... the Third Way is a political program for outsiders. It aims to disperse power and wipe out hierarchies at every opportunity.

Critics of the Third Way say its very pragmatism, its lack of an ideological core, together with its emphasis on dispersing power and direct democracy mean that it tends to dissolve into hollow spin, as seems to have happened in Blair's Britain. This may be one of the paradoxes of Latham. He is a conviction politician, but when I asked his colleagues what they thought was the core of this conviction – his *story* – they had no straightforward answer.

The Third Way, with its emphasis on dispersing power, provides an architecture for his natural "club-busting" inclinations, born of his life experience.

As I write, Mark Latham is under attack for not releasing key policies, particularly on tax and welfare. I believe that his books, which I will come to later, indicate the direction in which those policies might move. I am surprised so few political journalists seem to have looked at them.

I am prepared to make one prediction. When Australians go to the polls, they will have a clear idea of what they are voting for. I think that Latham in his policy speech will lay out exactly what he intends to do, just as Whitlam did in 1972. The question is whether Australia is ready for another program of social reform on the scale of Whitlam's – particularly after so many years in which voters have been conditioned to think mainly about economic management.

There is a further question. If he is elected, will the arc of Latham's government also resemble that of Whitlam's? Will he fail to manage? Will he be resisted? Will he crash and burn?

It is hard to re-imagine the Whitlam years. Hearing how things were done then is both strange and familiar, like looking at pictures of one's parents when young. The clothes are out of date, the poses look corny, the attitude all wrong, yet we can recognise our own bone structure, the delineation of our own potential.

I have a friend who remembers the night Gough Whitlam visited the central Queensland town of Emerald in November 1974. Emerald had television. Only five years before, the townsfolk had gathered in the few homes that had a set to watch Neil Armstrong land on the moon. They put blue cellophane over the screens to cut down on the "snow" and get a clearer picture. Since then, life had been changing fast. Coalmines had opened in the area, and the once solid Country Party community was divided between unionists and farmers. Most but not all houses had gained telephones. Meanwhile the only easily available newspaper, the *Central Queensland News*, reported intermittently and with some alarm on big changes happening down south. Emerald was beginning to feel like part of a larger world and the response was fear, resentment and a sense of broadening possibility.

My friend was just twenty, and had not yet voted in a federal election. He hadn't been able to go to university. The fees had been out of his parents' reach and he had gone straight from school into a job. Two years before, he had been preparing to go to Vietnam. He had had a heavy, fatalistic sense that his name would be drawn in the lottery of the call-up. He was opposed to the war, but draft dodging was not something he considered. That was what radicals did down south.

In Emerald there was no thought of civil disobedience, or even of political change; there was barely any vocabulary with which to discuss such things. The politics were, and always had been, those of place and of isolation. Ludwig Leichhardt had been the first European in the area. He named a local river the Comet after seeing a shooting star in the sky, and inscribed the word "dig" on a tree. Now Emerald lay a thousand kilometres from the state capital at the end of the long spur-line of road and rail that penetrated the inland from Rockhampton. Canberra was regarded as though it were the capital of a foreign land.

Now Gough Whitlam was coming to town, only the second prime minister in history to penetrate this part of Australia's interior. Whitlam had been re-elected earlier that year in a poll he was later to describe as the election everyone liked to forget he had won. He was visiting Emerald during a state election campaign. Whitlam's diary for that day, 29 November 1974, shows that he left Canberra early in the morning and had already been to Brisbane and to a civic reception in Clermont before flying to Emerald. He was welcomed at the airport by the Emerald Fife Band and a crowd of about a hundred who booed and cheered in equal proportions. Emerald had never seen political passion to compare.

That night, arc lights lit up the warm Queensland night and Whitlam spoke from the back of a truck at the town's racecourse. The *Central Queensland News* later estimated the crowd at more than 700, from a town of just below 6000. My friend remembers the crowd was split down the middle. The unionists stood on one side, and the Country Party supporters were on the other. A recently killed kangaroo had been laid in front of the stage with the sign "Please protect us – we will help you to destroy the graziers". Someone had brought a goat with a sign around its neck reading "I hear my Daddy's here". There were placards with messages such as "Gough We Never Had It So Bad". Another demanded "Telephones for the Brigalow Blocks" – a reference to the flat grazing country cleared of brigalow scrub a generation before, and still a country of struggle, loneliness, isolation and neglect.

One side of the crowd were chanting "We Want Joh." Whitlam responded, "Poor old Joh. Poor Old Joh." My friend remembers very little of what Whitlam said. Rather he remembers the excitement, the sudden revelation of strong feelings in a town he recollects mainly as dull and devoid of a sense of a larger purpose in life. He can't remember whether he felt awe or alarm. He consciously positioned himself in the middle, between the two political camps. He was, quite literally, not sure where he should stand.

The *Central Queensland News* reported that Whitlam's speech – constantly interrupted by jeers and heckling – veered between criticising the Premier, Joh Bjelke-Petersen, and promoting the record of the Whitlam government, particularly in supporting local councils. More money was coming to Queensland, Whitlam said, but Joh wasn't spending it in the right way. Whitlam talked about the problems of the area – high telephone costs, locust control and the beef road between Clermont and Charters Towers, which the federal government was paying to upgrade.

At the end of Whitlam's speech, the band prepared to play the new national anthem, "Advance Australia Fair", which had been introduced just a few months before. The crowd objected and asked for "God Save the Queen". As the band struck up, a group gathered and tried to drown out the new song with the old. Whitlam ignored them. Although it had been a very long day, he went from the racecourse to the Emerald Star Hotel's Railway Bar and shouted all comers to beer. It turned into an impromptu party.

A year after that visit to Emerald, at the general election held after his dismissal by Sir John Kerr, the electorates surrounding the town joined the rest of the nation in swinging hard against Labor. Gough was out. When he spoke at Emerald, his star was already in decline. He would be revered, cursed and remembered for decades. The prime ministers who came after him were all less alarming than Whitlam.

My friend doesn't remember how he cast his vote in 1975. Quite possibly it would have been for the Country Party candidate, because he was a good bloke and a hard-working local member, always a visible and approachable presence. In subsequent years my friend went to university, left Emerald, travelled the world and today works for a multinational company in information technology. He has led a very different life from that which seemed on offer in 1972.

The nature of political campaigning changed after Whitlam. By the 1980s, most homes had television, and politicians hardly ever stood on the back of trucks to be heckled and booed under arc lights. A new kind of stage-managed, professionalised, poll-driven politics developed. Street-walks and rallies were pieces of scripted theatre. The audience were not the audience at all, but part of the cast, carefully chosen. The real audience were remote, less connected with their neighbours, sitting in their lounge-rooms, with no blue cellophane over the screen.

Mark Latham has returned to the Whitlam style of campaigning – town-hall meetings away from what he describes as "the bubble" of Canberra. His staff describe these community meetings as a "secret weapon". The feeling is that Howard will never expose himself in quite the same way, and that if he did he would not perform well. But what does it mean, in 2004, to hold a community meeting? Surely it must mean very different things from what it did thirty years ago.

Latham has written about the need to re-invent the civic society, the kind of community in which people come together to achieve things. Television, he believes, is the enemy. In his book *Civilising Global Capital*, he wrote that when civil society was strong, "there was no such thing as a celebrity." Individuals were recognised for concrete things – actual contributions to local communities. The advent of television corresponds with the loss of civic engagement in Western nations:

> Never before has society left it to a commercial market (and the mass media cannot be properly understood as anything but commerce) to fashion its norms, values and sources of social recognition … As a society we used to convey messages by language and personal contact. Now we seem to interact as much with electronic technology as with each other.

This, he says, is a challenge not only for politicians but also for any citizen seeking to connect with others. It is a challenge for politics in the deepest sense of the word – how human beings are to organise themselves to live together.

Julia Gillard says Labor's present election campaign is being driven by Latham's ideas about "getting beyond the traditional forms of engagement with the community". His ideas are a mixture of the old and the new. He writes about the potential for the internet to provide a kind of direct democratic forum on issues where the parliament holds no special expertise, and which are naturally part of the community's concern – things such as national identity, whether or not the government should apologise to Aborigines, and the preamble to the constitution.

He also believes in the power of face-to-face contact. Latham's first speech to be broadcast on national television was his reply to the budget in mid-May. It was slammed by the political commentators as being too short on detail, particularly on tax. I think one of its most important elements was entirely overlooked by the insiders. Latham began his speech with these words:

> For the past five months I've been travelling around this great country of ours as Labor leader, talking to the Australian people about their concerns. It's been the experience of a lifetime. I've been holding community forums: old town-hall-style meetings, open to all comers. Thousands have come along to have their say – community leaders, school-teachers, small-business people, mums, dads and students. I call these meetings "democracy in the raw" – a chance to listen and learn, a chance to talk to people face-to-face. It's an important process, because as parliamentarians we need to be honest with ourselves. The Australian people have become disillusioned with the political process.
>
> We have lost their trust and confidence. And we need to regain it. Listening to people and addressing their concerns. Staying in touch with the real-life circumstances of the Australian people. Tonight I'm bringing those concerns and circumstances to Canberra. This is

what the people have been telling me. On the Central Coast of New South Wales they told me about the need to create new training and employment opportunities for the youth of the district. Plus put them in contact with mentors – role models who can point troubled teenagers in the right direction. At Gladstone in Central Queensland they told me about the need for more apprenticeships and group training opportunities – workforce skills for the next generation. In Brisbane I heard about the need for bulk-billing doctors and a national dental program – something positive to help our senior citizens get their teeth fixed up. In Adelaide I heard about the problems in the social security system: family debts and disincentives for people who want to move from welfare to work.

In the La Trobe Valley and Gippsland they told me about the loss of basic services, particularly in higher education and Medicare. At the community forum in Bairnsdale one man summarised what I've been hearing all over the country. He said that people were coming forward with "cries for help". Cries for increased social investment and better services. Cries for stronger communities and more lasting relationships. Cries for a fairer society – where by working hard and pulling together, we can give all Australians a fair go. Australia needs a government that answers this cry for help – a government that invests in its people and builds the services of a civilised society.

In the week after this speech was delivered, I rang a friend of mine, a suburban newspaper reporter, who had been at one of Latham's community meetings in Brisbane. How had his budget-in-reply speech gone down? She said to me, "They love it that he talked about them. That there he was in parliament, on television, and he reported back."

A month later Latham opened question time in parliament by asking Howard if he agreed that political leaders should have more face-to-face contact with the Australian people and, if so, whether he would accept a challenge to hold, not the standard election-campaign television debate, but rather a series of community forum debates. This question – which received a non-committal response – went almost unreported. The only mention I saw was to dismiss it as an attempt by Latham to distract from his commitment to withdraw the troops from Iraq by Christmas, and his failure to release a tax policy.

Meanwhile I was approaching Latham's office asking for an interview. I hoped for a number of encounters, but I would have settled for an hour, even half an hour, of his time.

I was refused. At first, with the arrogance common to my profession, I thought it must be a mistake – that the request had not been properly passed on or seriously considered. I tried again, and I pulled strings – the sort of strings only an insider could pull. I talked to Latham's publisher at Pluto Press, Evan Thornley, who put in a word for me with Latham's chief of staff, Mike Richards. I mentioned the matter to John Button, and to Julia Gillard. All this had absolutely no effect. The refusal was clearly a considered one. Latham's press secretary, Glenn Byres – highly professional, highly polished, the very model of a modern political spin doctor – told me that Latham was not doing "profile pieces". I told him this was not a personal profile, that I was interested in discussing Latham's ideas. "We are not doing sit-down, in-depth pieces," came the response. "I use the word 'profile' to mean anything sit-down and in-depth."

I assumed that my request for an interview was rejected because the audience of *Quarterly Essay* was not Latham's priority. He was trying to talk to the outsiders – those who rarely read "sit-down, in-depth" newspapers, let alone essays of this kind.

Still stinging from rejection and in the process of drafting yet another request, I asked the editor of *Quarterly Essay*, Chris Feik, for information about the readership. He replied that the last few issues had sold over 9000 copies, and that there were more than 1000 subscribers. "As for demographics, who can afford to ascertain such a thing? Whether our readers are all latte-sipping enemies of the people is hard to say. One assumes not."

Latham has written about the educated, left-leaning middle class. This was largely created, he has said, by Gough Whitlam's reforms, including free tertiary education and better public broadcasting.

After Whitlam the Labor Party became an uneasy alliance between the educated middle class and the workers. Whitlam's reforms had created "a new generation of insiders" – the progressive establishment, led by academics and artists. For Latham, the culture wars of recent times have their origin in the old elite's resentment of the new "insiders".

In reality, he says, the two groups have a lot in common. Both talk in abstracts. He compares the journalist Phillip Adams, usually seen as being on the left, with Piers Akerman, the notoriously intemperate right-wing columnist for Sydney's *Daily Telegraph*. Both are insiders, part of the media elite. Both live within a few blocks of each other in affluent, inner-Sydney Paddington.

> They have little experience of suburban life and suburban values. Both practise a symbolic and abstract style of politics, based on the concentration of power and the preservation of the ruling elite. They are both out of touch.

The crisis of Labor in recent years is that the alliance between the educated middle class and the workers lies in ruins. Evan Thornley, a Labor Party insider and the publisher of some of Latham's books, uses the terms "academics" and "punters" to describe the two sides of the fracture. Latham has coined more confronting terms. He speaks of "Tourists" and "Residents". He says the insiders live like tourists in their own country. There is a sense in which they don't live in Australia at all.

> They travel extensively, eat out, and buy in domestic help. They

see the challenges of globalisation as an opportunity, a chance to further develop their identity and information skills. This abstract lifestyle has produced an abstract style of politics. Symbolic and ideological campaigns are given top priority. This involves a particular methodology: adopting a predetermined position on issues and then looking for evidence to support that position.

The outsiders, on the other hand – the people who live in the outer suburbs and the regions – are the Residents of Australia. Their values are pragmatic. They cannot distance themselves from the problems of the neighbourhood, and so good behaviour and good services are all-important. There is no symbolism, and also no dogma, in the suburbs, Latham says. The Residents look for small, pragmatic improvements, and they are not interested in "big pictures".

Today Labor insiders tend to blame Paul Keating as much as John Howard for the ruin of the alliance between workers and intellectuals. Keating was hated in the suburbs. During the years of his government, Tourists were able to believe that the country was moving forward on issues like Aboriginal reconciliation, the Republic and social tolerance. What has happened since then – a defeated referendum and the xenophobia that accompanied the arrival of the *Tampa* – has been a reality check. The Residents haven't moved at all. Enough of the people now called Howard's battlers moved against Keating to deliver the Coalition victory in the 1996 election. By 2001 – the *Tampa* election – Howard had used the refugee issue to drive a wedge through the heart of the Australian Labor Party.

The academic David Burchell has noted that the most atypical Australians, as measured by their attitudes to immigration, multiculturalism and ethnicity, are the graduates of the universities. In their attitudes and beliefs they are "foreign" to their fellow Australians.

The 2001 Australian Election Survey, conducted by political scientists at the Australian National University, showed that only one in five

Australians disagreed that asylum seekers should be turned back. But 44 per cent of graduates were against turning them back. Twice as many graduates as other Australians disagreed with the statement that migrants should try to be "more Australian". Overall, Australians supported the return of the death penalty by more than two to one. Among graduates, the proportions were reversed. The residents of western Sydney – home of the Howard battlers that delivered him power – varied from national opinion on seven key questions of migration, multiculturalism and national identity by just nine percentage points. Graduates differed from the rest of Australia by almost eighteen percentage points – in the opposite direction.

Some of those in Latham's inner circle refer to the favoured issues of the Tourists – such as refugees and Aboriginal reconciliation – as "totems". In their view, the left-intellectual approach to these issues is built on faith and conviction more than on reason, let alone political pragmatics. If Labor lets down the Tourists on these matters, the party will be denounced as betraying its true values. Yet the people Labor needs to win back – the Residents – are either hostile or indifferent.

Evan Thornley said to me, "I don't want to reduce it all to numbers, because I am aware of the moral element, but how many asylum seekers are there? At most a few thousand. And how many people's lives are blighted by unemployment? Many, many more. Generations of families, and neither of Labor's factional machines seems to care enough to focus much on it." Thornley argues that unemployment is the sleeper issue, waiting to hit any government hard. "Our real unemployment rate is not 5.6 per cent, contrary to what you've been breathlessly told by government and media. The numbers are a fraud. If you add up the numbers of unemployment, disability and sole parent benefits, there are more people now than there were ten years ago, despite a decade of boom. We've just re-arranged the deckchairs." Unemployment will double, Thornley says, if there is another recession, and this seems likely. We have economic growth, but also rocketing consumer debt. "We have the best party on the block because we've borrowed more money to buy more beer." These are the sorts of issues, Thornley argues, with which the "academics" should be engaging.

Julia Gillard is optimistic about the party's ability to heal the alliance between Tourists and Residents. Already, she says, many of the Tourists have shifted, forced by the 2001 election to realise how far removed their views are from those of the majority. As Opposition Spokeswoman on Immigration, she crafted the Labor Party's policy on asylum seekers. It was a compromise, including mandatory detention for limited periods in supervised, hostel-style accommodation, and a more compassionate approach to holders of Temporary Protection Visas. The most helpful people in the process of drafting the policy, she says, were those who believed passionately in the injustice of mandatory detention but who recognised the need for policy to be politically sellable.

Left-wing totemism is on the decline in Latham's Labor. This doesn't necessarily mean, Gillard says, that the Tourists will be ignored. Tourists and Residents agree on some things; both tend to believe that Australian foreign policy should be home-grown, for example. In early August, Latham's brinkmanship over the Free Trade Agreement with the United States delivered another example: both insiders and outsiders are likely to be pleased with Labor's moves to protect Australian content rules in broadcasting, and to safeguard the Pharmaceutical Benefits Scheme from big drug companies. Latham's tactics, on this issue at least, showed a shrewd understanding of what it might take to bind Labor's two constituencies. More broadly, Gillard believes that the more Labor addresses the direct concerns of the Residents, the more congenial the climate will be for the Tourists.

I was sore from Latham's rejection, even though I soon confirmed that it was not personal. All journalists who took a "sit-down, in-depth" approach were getting the same response in May, June and early July 2004. Meanwhile Latham appeared on Rove McManus's variety show and on *Burke's Backyard*. The former Victorian premier, Joan Kirner, who has – almost to her own surprise – become a Latham supporter, suggested to me that Latham didn't want to be fully known. He wanted to project only facets of himself into the electorate.

I assumed that Mark Latham's refusal to deal with certain sections of the media answered one of the questions that I would have asked him. I wanted to know whether he was hostile to the middle-class Left. Did he really see us, to use Chris Feik's words, as "latte-sipping enemies of the people", or was he simply appealing to us to "get real", to become more connected? Would he continue the Howard government's practice of deriding intellectuals? It seemed through May and June that he didn't want to talk to us at all. The interview for *Quarterly Essay*, Glenn Byres told me when I demanded written reasons for the rejection, was "not a priority against competing demands on the eve of the election".

I recalled conversations with friends in 2001, during the *Tampa* affair, in which they talked, only half-joking, about wanting to leave the country. Perhaps New Zealand would be more politically palatable, they suggested. I used to get angry. I hadn't read Mark Latham's ideas then. Indeed, his most recent books had not yet been written. If I had known of his division between Tourists and Residents, I might have been tempted to think of my friends as rather tenuous Australians. I remembered when I lived in Queensland during the final days of the Bjelke-Petersen regime. Activism and opposition were a real risk to career and even to personal safety and privacy. I had asked the then head of the Council of Civil Liberties, Matt Foley (later to become a minister in the Goss Labor government), why he didn't move south, to a more temperate political climate. He had replied: "Because it's my state too."

I had fumed over lattes, sometimes, while friends discussed that great euphemism, Aboriginal disadvantage, as though it were only a question of rights and racism and not of children dying. For anyone who has seen the homicidal communities in remote Australia, and the children who are growing up illiterate – and therefore powerless – when their grandparents could read, it has been clear for some time that the policies of the Left have been far too abstract for far too long. Nor is this only the Left's failure. Until Howard, Aboriginal policy was mostly bipartisan. Abstract politics, out of touch with reality, created a moral vacuum into which the assimilationists have moved.

Two years ago the Aboriginal academic Marcia Langton published a scorching attack on the Left in *Overland* magazine. Left-wingers who saw themselves as the defenders of Aborigines did not know what they were talking about, she said, and their attitudes of moral superiority to the Howard government were not supported by the facts. Langton said she had abandoned any hope that the Left could provide Aboriginal people with useful support. "The Left has a romantic set of universal values, such as solidarity and brotherhood, but outside the urban Western café society where ideas have few consequences, these concepts disappoint. They let people down." She said Aboriginal people living in rural Australia had more points of connection with Pauline Hanson's supporters than they did with city-based leftists.

> The poor white trash whom Pauline purported to represent are my nemesis and your food for thought. Their problems are my problems, and not yours … Aborigines and remote area graziers have one thing in common that no one can take away from us – poverty. Australia's urban Left has no purchase on this problem.

I reported on Langton's remarks for the *Age* and waited with interest for the response. The only response I saw was another article in a left-wing magazine, which concentrated entirely on attacking *Quadrant* magazine for publishing right-wing material and defending the publishing record of left-wing magazines. It made me want to scream. As my friend, the anthropologist Peter Sutton, remarked: "*Quadrant* and *Overland* would be very useful on Cape York. They lack toilet paper up there."

If Latham was saying to the intellectual elite that they should "get real" – become less abstract, less dogmatic and more engaged, then I could agree with him. If he was going to continue the denigration of the "elite" that had marked the Howard years, then I could not. If he was going to behave as though morality was only a matter of numbers and pragmatics, then I would not be able to follow. It is a strange and unhealthy country that tries to exclude and vilify its thinkers, and it is a sad and diminished imagination that cannot grasp that symbols, story and culture are also important, including but not only for Aboriginal people.

Latham is certainly not anti-intellectual. He has written books. He has said that education should be the nation's first priority, and teaching at all levels an honoured profession. But he is undoubtedly against abstract thinking. He wrote in 1997, reflecting on the defeat of the Keating government, that the "chattering classes" were Labor's hangers-on and the party would be stronger without them. He wrote that in government Labor had become too civilised and not radical enough. "If being civilised means patronising the high arts more than public housing estates, Labor needs less of it."

In his more recent writing, Latham has refined but hardly softened these ideas. In his 2002 Menzies Lecture, he spoke of the need for Labor to develop a "radical edge" by combining Labor thinking with outsider concerns:

> As a political movement our values and instincts are still sound: defending the underdog, fighting for unfashionable causes, protecting the less privileged. The challenge is to project these values beyond the economic debate and into the sphere of public culture … wherever power and privilege are concentrated in society – whether in the boardrooms of big business, the pretensions of big media, the political manipulation of big churches or the arrogance of big bureaucracies – we need to be anti-establishment. The outsiders want us to shake the tree, take on the system on their behalf. They want us to break down the powerful centre of society and disperse influence and opportunity as widely as possible. This is

the logical consequence of having a better educated and informed
electorate ... we have entered an era of institutional rebellion.

Latham has used the phrase the "forgotten people" to describe the outsiders, and to describe those who earn incomes of less than $52,000, the
people who missed out on tax cuts in Howard's 2004 budget. Howard
was outraged – or feigned outrage – at Latham's use of this phrase, suggesting he was plagiarising Robert Menzies's famous 1942 "forgotten
people" speech.

In that speech, Menzies described society as being made up of three
layers. The upper class was made up of "the rich and powerful – those
who control great funds and enterprises and are as a rule able to protect
themselves". The working class was "the mass of unskilled people,
almost invariably well-organised and with their wages and conditions
safeguarded by popular law". The middle class – the forgotten people –
provided "the intellectual life which marks us off from the beast; the life
which finds room for literature, for the arts, for science, for medicine
and the law. This middle class maintains and fills the high schools and
universities and so feeds the lamp of learning."

There are two interesting counterpoints – almost ironies – in the
ways Menzies and Latham describe their forgotten people. Menzies saw
abstract ideas and values as virtues. He suggested that these were the
things that "mark us off from the beast" and make us human. He also saw
them as residing among the "outsiders" of his time – the middle class.
Today, according to Latham, abstract thought is at best irrelevant and at
worst an enormous political problem. In his analysis, it is the province of
the "insiders". Both men value education – "the lamp of learning" –
although for different reasons.

Gough Whitlam once wrote that the purpose of a Labor government's
agenda was "the creation of a society in which the arts and the apprecia-
tion of spiritual and intellectual values can flourish. Our other objectives
are all means to an end; the enjoyment of the arts is an end in itself."

It seems to me that in this, Whitlam and Menzies have more in common than Whitlam and Latham. Both Whitlam and Menzies were born into comfort and privilege and took education if not for granted, then certainly as part of their birthright. Both saw what Shirley Hazzard would call the "inattestable things" of life as essential, and as ends in themselves. Both Whitlam and Menzies, on Latham's analysis of society, would have been insiders, or Tourists.

Nor is it entirely true to say – as Latham has – that the difference between Whitlam and Menzies was that Whitlam believed in social mobility, while Menzies did not. It is often forgotten that Menzies was the first prime ministerial educational reformer. He opened up the universities, forcing them to engage with the community. He was the first to commit Commonwealth money to expand the system. He established new universities with an emphasis on teaching rather than pure research, and he made it possible for students to access the new places through a generous Commonwealth scholarship scheme. Mal Logan, the former vice-chancellor of Monash University, has argued that Menzies and Whitlam are part of the same tradition in education. He has said that the present Liberal government's policies – increasing fees and introducing full-fee places – mark an ideological retreat and a profound break with the trends of the last forty years.

Latham differs from Whitlam and Menzies in having been born on the fringes. He was lucky to get a good education, and it was never taken for granted. So far as one can judge from his written work, he sees education and the life of the mind as worthwhile not as ends in themselves but as means to social mobility and a more internationally competitive society.

If Latham is to win government, he clearly has to win back Howard's battlers. To do this, he talks values, and he talks education, and he talks social mobility. He does not talk about symbols or inattestable things, and he doesn't talk to Quarterly Essay.

But if he is to succeed in history then it seems to me that symbolism, if not dogma, must also be important.

Latham's understanding of the political divide that separates outsiders and insiders is, I think, one of his most powerful political weapons. It is born of his personal experience, and influenced by his personality. Who can doubt that it is the best model – probably *the* model – for understanding the last ten years of Australian politics? But it is only a model. Applied to any specific group other than the most extremely disadvantaged, it begins to wane in power. We are all insiders in some contexts, yet alienated outsiders in others. Many of the insiders are themselves the product of social mobility, and retain strong family links to outsider lifestyles. I suspect that in time this model will become both Latham's greatest strength and his greatest weakness.

That night thirty years ago in Emerald, few people remembered what Whitlam said. What they remembered were the symbols, and the new national anthem, and the futile attempt of the crowd to drown it out with "God Save the Queen". Looking back, it is the symbols, rather than the pragmatics, that tell us on which side the future lay.

It was clear that the only way I was going to see Mark Latham was to attend one of his community forums. The opportunity came on 19 May, the week after the budget and his speech in reply. Latham was travelling in Queensland between parliamentary sittings and would meet the people in Caboolture, on the northern fringes of Brisbane and in the marginal, Liberal-held seat of Longman. This was one of the seats that would have to change hands if Labor were to win power. Caboolture is close enough to the city to be a long commute, but far enough away to have the feeling of a country town. It is part of Australia's suburban fringe.

I arrived early and read the local papers in a coffee shop near the hall where the meeting was to be held. They were still carrying the budget coverage, being weekly papers. They emphasised that people on incomes of under $53,000 would not get tax cuts. That meant, said the *Caboolture News*, that 94 per cent of Longman residents would miss out. The coverage appeared on page eight of the newspaper. It was hardly the main story.

The front pages of the region's newspapers were taken up with the morality tales of community life. Businesses wanted council to impose a levy to pay for more security on the tourist strip. A teenage driver had been fined $120 for a noisy stereo. A local school had won an award for excellence. Students at the Caboolture campus of the University of Technology were complaining they were the "poor cousins" of the city campus and lacked resources. A study had shown a low-carbohydrate diet was a more efficient way of losing weight than a low-fat diet. This last story was sourced from Philadelphia, but got page three treatment – greater prominence than the Australian budget.

Security, quality of life, education and health. If Mark Latham had read the papers, he could only have been reassured that he was "on message" for these voters.

Sitting in the window of the coffee shop, I had a view up and down the main street. I could see three different employment agencies touting for business. As the hour for the community meeting drew near, it became clear that I was not the only visitor in town. A few other journalists arrived, and some political staffers. All of us stood out. We had been to the hairdresser's too recently. We wore too much black. These weren't the only distinguishing features. There was something else – in the posture, the facial expressions – some other hard-to-define but nevertheless tangible difference between those who were here because Mark Latham was here, and those who called Caboolture home. I couldn't tell the journalists and the political staffers apart, but I could tell at a glance the visitors from the residents.

Inside the hall there were rows of plastic chairs. There was an urn and thick white china cups laid out on a table. At the front a banner on stage read "Mark Latham and Labor – Opportunity for All". In front of this – not on stage but on the same level as the audience – was a microphone and a lectern for Latham, and another microphone to one side for members of the public to ask questions. The hall looked stripped-down, bare. The political staffers had disappeared. People drifted in. Soon the chairs were all full, and people stood three-deep around the sides. The Labor Party had advertised by direct mail to everyone in the electorate.

Latham arrived. He looked like a man who had put a suit on for a purpose, rather than someone for whom it was natural attire. There was nothing in his manner or appearance that led you to suppose he had written books, or that in them he had drawn upon philosophers ranging from Locke, Rousseau and Kant to John Rawls. He appeared in person much as he did on television – big, boofy even when well groomed – like a version of Ginger Meggs grown up and gone into politics.

He spoke briefly, and began by telling people that he had used his budget-in-reply speech the week before to report back from the community forums. He told the crowd he had been criticised for talking about vaccinating children and reading to babies, and that the government wanted to know when he was going to talk about the big issues. But children *were* the big issue, he said, with a nice show of passion. Then he invited the crowd to give him and Labor "a pat on the back or a kick in the shins", and took questions.

The queue of people waiting to speak stretched around the hall. Two hours later, when Latham stopped taking questions, it was not much shorter. There were questions about what he would do to help parents deal with wayward teenagers, and questions about the unemployed who spent the days lying around on the beaches. Latham repeated, from his budget speech, his "earning or learning" line as the options for young people. The crowd applauded. One man waited for more than an hour to ask, with evident frustration, a question he said he had been posing for fifty years. Why wasn't there a scheme to turn the rivers of eastern seaboard back to the centre of the continent, to water the desert? Latham replied, without breaking stride, that the reason for this was that the best scientific advice suggested it wasn't a good idea. There were questions on the aged pension – and on the problems of self-funded retirees who were "not living, just existing" on their meagre savings. These were things, Latham said, he could not do much about at present. In compensation he offered Labor's dental program, under which pensioners would be able to get their teeth fixed up for free. One of the people at the microphone opened his mouth so that Latham, the alternative prime minister, could see the work that needed to be done.

Halfway through the forum I wrote in my notebook, "He uses no rhetoric. The people do." All the passion, the high-flown language, was coming not from Latham but from the crowd. They were eloquent. They, if not Latham, had a keen sense of symbolism.

An elderly woman took the microphone. She told Latham her name was Maree Newman, and she represented the local branch of a national society of grandparents who cared for grandchildren when their parents were unable or unwilling to do so. She reminded Latham of another community meeting in New South Wales, at which he had spoken to another member of her group who had had her grandchildren with her.

"You said to our member, who was trying to reach you through the crowd, you said 'Let the lady and her children through.' I thank you for that." It was almost biblical. "Suffer the little children …" I found myself thinking, and I smiled. Latham responded in the same unflappable, matter-of-fact way that he had to the man who wanted to turn the rivers back to the inland. He certainly didn't look like a Messiah.

Maree Newman was warming up. She carried the kind of natural authority that stilled a room. She was a matriarch, and a great political speaker. She gave him a list of the people she was helping to care for — her grandchildren, her sick husband, her failing parents and her own middle-aged, mentally disabled child. There was respite care and back-up to help with all of these people except for her grandchildren. Who would look after them if she became sick or died? She talked about grandparents who had lost their homes to finance Family Court fights to gain custody of children at risk. She told him that grandparents were often the first to know when there were problems in a family, but they received no help. Nobody knew how many of them were caring for grandchildren because Centrelink did not keep figures. She told Mark Latham she wanted a package of measures to help. She wanted legal aid for grandparents before the Family Court, and a non-means-tested Centrelink payment at least equivalent to that received by foster parents. Latham listened in silence, then took from her a portfolio of material and said he would get back to her.

When the forum was over, I asked Maree Newman to let me know if she ever heard back from Latham or his people. Nearly four weeks later she rang me. She had that morning taken a personal call from Mark Latham. At first she had thought it must be a joke, but soon she recognised his voice – the unmistakeable flat vowels and matter-of-fact intonation. He told her he was picking up her proposals as Labor Party policy, and would announce them later in the election campaign. He was arranging for her to meet Wayne Swan, the Shadow Minister for Family and Community Services, to iron out the details. Before she rang me, Maree Newman had been telephoning around the country to all the branches of her organisation, telling grandparents that it was now up to them to make sure that Mark Latham was elected. Not a word of this appeared in any media reports following the Caboolture forum.

In the weeks that followed my trip to Caboolture, I contacted suburban newspaper reporters around Australia who had covered his other forums. None of them was in any doubt that he was winning votes. In Pakenham, on the edge of Melbourne, he had promised that a Labor federal government would fund a $21 million shortfall for the Pakenham bypass. This alone, the reporter thought, might have won him the seat. In the northern suburbs of Adelaide, in April, he had said, in response to questions, that a Labor government would consider fully funding the vaccine for the deadly pneumococcal virus – a move he later confirmed as one of his promises in his budget-in-reply speech. The people of the northern suburbs of Adelaide took this to mean he had listened to them. They saw it as their idea, picked up by Mark Latham and taken to parliament. Everywhere he got brownie points just for showing up. "It's the way he shows up too," one reporter said. "The way his big bus pulls up outside the hall. I mean, it's not a shiny government car."

That day in Caboolture Mark Latham was on his feet responding to questions for two hours. When the meeting time was up, he sat down and spoke to people individually for another hour. It was an exhausting, marathon performance. I felt tired just watching it.

I had been asking for only an hour of his time, and would have settled for less.

There was no way to feel, that day, other than humble. Latham's performance, particularly his handling of Maree Newman, was smart politics. The minders and the spin doctors were with him, of course, but they stayed so far out of sight during the meeting that I had trouble finding them later. His performance was not only smart. It was impossible to doubt his sincerity in connecting with his "outsiders". And it was clear that even in the television age, face-to-face, town-hall campaigning was still powerful in ways both familiar and new. Perhaps it is all the more powerful because society generally lacks civic connectedness.

How much good will it do Mark Latham? Perhaps not enough. People who turn up at community forums may not be representative of the broader electorate. They are already engaged with the political process. Many of the audience members I spoke to were disillusioned Labor voters – the kind of people who had stuck with Labor, resentfully, through the Keating years. Now they felt the party was "back on track". Perhaps Latham will achieve a lift in the hearts of traditional Labor voters without winning seats.

There are limits to what community forums can achieve. That day there were no questions on abstracts, and none on the national economy writ large. Nevertheless I suspect that most voters worry about these things, even if they lack the vocabulary and don't feel qualified to quiz a leader on the finer points. The outsiders in seats like Longman may agree with Latham that the real issues are social, yet still want the economy to be run by someone who seems to understand it.

Quizzing leaders on the technicalities and the abstracts is the natural role of insiders, including journalists who are meant to serve the public. One of my friends – another journalist – suggested that the correct thing for me to have done that day was to have taken the microphone and asked my journalist's questions in that way. I was horrified by the suggestion, but it took me a while to analyse why.

To have taken the microphone – to have asked, among that crowd waiting for hours to speak, about his books, about whether he is for or against the intellectual elite and about the legacy of Gough, even about the economy writ large – would have been an act of the most extraordinary arrogance. Journalists assume the right to question people, to take up their time, on the grounds that we are serving the public. But if I had seized the microphone on that day, I would have been doing the exact reverse of this. I would have taken time from people who had just one opportunity to talk to a key politician about their struggle to survive on a pension, their worries about their children, and their teeth.

It is clear to me that one of the changes Mark Latham has already brought to politics is an intense challenge to the media's sense of self-importance. Almost every one of the political moves and tactics that mattered to the people at the community forums – the "report back" in the budget speech, the apparent picking up of the immunisation idea, the challenge to the Prime Minister to have community forum debates rather than a television debate – were missed or dismissed by the national political insiders, but picked up and reported in local newspapers and radio stations.

This could be forgiven if the national media had focussed instead on the architecture of Latham's ideas – the big messages in his books. These are material enough for critique and controversy.

But that didn't happen either. Instead the national political media showed that denied their usual provender, they will find some other way to feed.

CHARACTER

By late May, I had spent a considerable amount of time researching Mark Latham's past, in particular his time as Labor mayor of Liverpool in Sydney's south-west. I knew he had enemies for whom it had become a personal mission to damage him. I had been given a file of clippings and other material described as "the dirt". Much of the same material had already been given to the *Age* journalists Malcolm Schmidtke and Gay Alcorn for a March profile article, and to the *Daily Telegraph* columnist Piers Akerman. It was available to anyone who asked.

The *Age* reporters had assessed the material and decided there was little of substance in it. I came to the same conclusion. Certainly, there were insights into Latham's character: it was clear he had been rude, even cruel, to his predecessors and his rivals. There was information on pre-selection battles – allegations and counter-allegations of branch-stacking – though nothing implicating Latham directly. None of it added up to much more than a life lived in the political maelstrom that was Liverpool Labor. The dirt file was fatally damaging only in the eyes of those who had already condemned Mark Latham. All of it has become public since I was in his hometown in May.

Before the mid-2004 frenzy, some "dirt" about Mark Latham was already on the public record. The story most people seemed to know about him was that he had broken a taxi driver's arm. The *Australian* had interviewed the taxi driver shortly after Latham was elected Labor leader in December 2003. Latham was in the taxi riding home from Gough Whitlam's eighty-fifth birthday in Darling Harbour. He accused the driver, Bachir Mustafa, of taking a roundabout route to Bankstown. They argued, and Latham refused to pay the fair. Mustafa snatched his bag and ran away with it, and Latham rugby-tackled him. Mustafa broke his arm in the fall. Not surprisingly, neither Latham nor Mustafa pressed charges. The *Australian* quoted Mustafa as saying, "I've got no grudge against him. Good luck to him with his new position. Nobody is perfect and we all make mistakes." He said Latham was a man to "stand up for his rights. Every time I answered him back, he says, 'Rubbish.'" If the Liberal Party had been hoping for political capital from the taxi driver, it seemed they would be disappointed.

The *Age* had also reported in their profile that another man in Liverpool claimed to have been assaulted by Latham. I didn't have time to follow this up before the course of the phoney federal election campaign radically altered, and events overtook me.

On Thursday, 1 July, about six weeks after my trip to Liverpool, I received a call from an old friend, a member of the Labor Party and a media "insider". She knew I was working on this essay, and she had just heard something she thought I would like to check out. Journalists had told her that the Channel Nine *Sunday* program, due to air that weekend, had a video of Mark Latham's buck's night. The video was said to show something that, if broadcast, would finish him. Howard could be expected to call the election for 7 August – the soonest possible date.

The next day – Friday – I spoke to another friend who holds a senior post in News Limited. He told me that the *Herald-Sun* reporter Lincoln Wright had interviewed Gabrielle Gwyther, and she had alleged that Mark Latham had been domestically violent. I told my friend I had spoken to Gwyther, and she had denied similar rumours. "He's got her on tape," my friend said. "It's on the record."

I had interviewed Latham's ex-wife, Gabrielle Gwyther, in early June. This was before she hit the national headlines, although she had been spoken to by the *Age* journalists. Gwyther had told them the same thing she told me: that Latham had a controlling personality, that he was narcissistic, that she had at times felt intimidated by him, but she emphasised that he had never been physically violent.

Now I began to doubt whether I had it right. I rang Gwyther again to put the rumour to her directly. She vigorously denied it. She would never have stayed with Latham if he had been violent, she said. His intimidation had been subtler. She had only realised its extent and effect since the relationship ended. She told me she had spoken to other journalists to give them "just little bits, a bit more psychological insight into him", but that this had not included anything like allegations of domestic violence. I asked her about the buck's night. She said it had been organised by people who were not close friends, and Latham had just turned up. She gathered it had been embarrassing in the way that buck's nights are, but she didn't know any details. She had never heard anything about a video. I rang the man whom she said had organised the night. He didn't want to talk.

I was wondering what else I had missed, and just how badly I was about to be scooped. Chris Feik and I had a conversation in which we agreed that this essay might turn out to be a reflection on what could have been. If the video were to be aired, Latham would be finished and the election over before we could publish.

By now, Channel Nine was promoting the *Sunday* program. The promotions made it clear that *Sunday* had tracked down Don Nelson, the other man who claimed to have been assaulted by Latham.

After months of refusing media interview requests, Latham went on the John Laws radio program on Friday morning to address the Nelson allegations. They were not true, he said, and there was nothing new in them. It had all been published before, and denied by him, in the *Age* profile. It had happened fifteen years ago in the Labor Party campaign rooms, and it had been Nelson who had "taken a half-swing at me ... We grabbed him and got him out of the campaign rooms."

Laws asked, "Did you biff him?"

Latham said, "No, no, I grabbed hold of him. He was – I mean, not in any state to do anyone real harm, but we just got hold of him and got him out of the campaign rooms. A bit of crowd control, and that was the end of that."

Meanwhile the allegations about the video had become common knowledge among journalists – among the insiders – but had yet to break publicly. For those in the know, little snippets and indications were popping up all over the place. Laws raised "suggestions" that Latham had had a sex life between his marriages. Latham made a joke of it: "Can I just give you the breaking news? I had an active love life before marriage! Now, imagine what the Liberal Party will do with that! I can hardly wait for Tony Abbott's diatribe in the Australian Parliament – ooh, what a person!"

Current-affairs programs made veiled references to "other" things that were to be aired on Sunday. The editorial in the Australian contained a veiled reference: "allegations that Mr Latham might have got physical, in different ways with different people". The media was engaged in an exercise of nudge and wink. I was a long way from the Canberra press gallery, but I could feel the heat from fever.

By Friday afternoon, the internet gossip site crikey.com.au became the first to go public, referring to "rumours of a potentially embarrassing videotape of Latham's buck's party ahead of his last wedding", and noted that John Laws had asked "the rather bizarre question about whether Latham had an active sex life between marriages. Hmmm, is this somehow connected to the buck's video? Who knows?"

Soon Crikey had good company. In Saturday's Sydney Morning Herald, Canberra journalist Louise Dodson wrote, "The Labor leader is yet to respond to other revelations – reports of a raunchy video taken at his buck's night before his second marriage."

The video had been elevated from a "rumour" in Crikey to a "report" and a "revelation" in the ostensibly more reputable Sydney Morning Herald. Meanwhile the executive producer of the Sunday show, John Lyons, was telling the reporters who rang to check that Sunday did not have a video, and that even if they did they wouldn't use it. But not everyone checked.

Finally Sunday dawned. I doubt if there were many reporters in the country who did not get up early. News Limited newspapers were running Lincoln Wright's story about Gwyther. It made no allegations of domestic violence, but was written and headlined in such a way that the superficial reader would come away with the impression Latham was a wife-batterer.

The quotes were not attributed to Gwyther, but to "friends" of hers. A News Limited source told me later that Gwyther had been "on the record" with Wright, but at the last minute had lost her nerve and asked if he could attribute the story to her "friends". Heaven knows why. The article merely repeated in more detail the things she had already told the *Age* in March.

At last the *Sunday* program aired. Latham's enemies from Liverpool City Council were interviewed, and the most telling parts of the "dirt file" were used. Don Nelson made his allegations and called Latham a liar for denying the assault. Supporters of Latham were also interviewed. As a whole the program was balanced. There was no knockout blow, no sign of a video, and nothing I had not already known.

I rang my original source, and we speculated on what had happened to the video. Did it exist? Would it be used later in the campaign? I was wondering how I would write about all this, if no video had emerged by the time *Quarterly Essay* went to print. Could I mention it at all?

The next day, on Monday afternoon, Latham called a press conference to tackle the rumours. Latham said: "There is no video – it was a buck's night, which was tame enough. It was organised by other people. I turned up. I had a buck's night for the first marriage and, believe you me, I didn't see the need for it the second time around. It was tame enough and there's nothing there I would be embarrassed about, but there's no video."

He choked up when begging the press gallery to leave his family alone. Among the reporters, it was hard to say which feeling was dominant – excitement at tears from the alternative prime minister, or the dawning realisation that there was not, and never had been, a video.

Latham aired for the first time gossip that was new to me – that he was a sexual harasser. He denied it: "This rumour has circulated for six years. I wouldn't know the name of the person, the nature of the incident, any of that detail. I know it didn't happen, and no one has ever been able to put to me anything other than the nature of the rumour … it is like trying to grab hold of a puff of smoke; it doesn't exist."

He blamed all the rumours about his personal life on three sources: "the first wife", his old enemies in Liverpool, and a Liberal Party smear unit.

Of his marriage break-up, he said: "It was hard; it was messy. I would've made mistakes. I mean, there were things that you just wouldn't believe. It's the toughest part of your life. If anyone has had a perfect marriage break-up, let me know about it – I don't think anyone ever has."

A few days later, the *Sydney Morning Herald* ran an article about Mark Latham by the reporters Damien Murphy and Deborah Snow. It included more comments from Gwyther, including an allegation – denied by him – that Latham had played a pornographic video at a family function to embarrass her parents. It also alleged that Latham used his job with Gough Whitlam to try to impress women, and that he had made an advance to one woman after hours in Whitlam's office and had been rejected. The *Australian*'s columnist Matt Price was later to remark that the article was "a stand-out disgrace". I think it was all of that, but – worse still – irrelevant. When, I wondered, was anyone going to read Latham's books and expose some of his ideas to public scrutiny?

In the whole affair, nothing of substance about Latham had been exposed that had not been published before, by the *Age*, in March 2004. If anything had been revealed about Latham's character, it was to be found in the way he had handled the rumours rather than in what the media had published. I thought about a passage in one of his books. Latham had quoted Paul Keating's comparison of politics with pedalling a bicycle, and written: "Let me take the analogy further. When a bike starts moving, it wobbles from side to side. The rider then has a choice: to stop the bike or to pedal faster. I'm a great believer in always pedalling faster." Latham had pedalled faster. It seemed to me to be an illuminating way of thinking about several of his erratic and creative moves, including his handling of the Free Trade Agreement, over which his party seemed impossibly split, as the phoney election campaign continued.

On the Saturday of the weekend when the famous non-existent video was meant to be screened, News Limited papers carried a column by

Glenn Milne, who canvassed what Gwyther had said about Latham being intimidating, and went on to write:

> Over the past forty-eight hours there's been fevered speculation in Canberra about the existence of a raunchy buck's night video involving Mr Latham – and whether that was the smoking gun about to be fired by *Sunday*. Frankly, this was always going to happen. It was just a matter of time. Political insiders have been aware of several untested stories about Mr Latham's attitude to women. Running for the prime ministership means your private life inevitably belongs to the nation. It is the price of office. Fairly or unfairly, Mr Latham is now undergoing this test by fire. And precisely because Prime Minister John Howard wants to see how Mr Latham emerges from the controversy, he won't be calling an August 7 election. He now senses the Labor leader may be starting to unravel. Whether that's wishful thinking or not, it's a fact that several elements of the dramatic pre-election story unfolding in Canberra are now about to converge.

In retrospect, Milne's article is almost funny. Guns that have not yet been fired but that are nevertheless smoking, tests by fire that are the price of office, unravelling leaders and dramatic stories unfolding and converging at the same time. At least Crikey peddled its gossip in plain prose. Milne's article was written in a way which suggested revelation and legitimate journalistic inquiry, but which in fact obscured and confused. For me, it symbolised the whole grubby affair.

What conclusions can we draw about character from these events? I will sum up what is now on the public record, and the conclusions I have drawn from my own research.

Latham was brought up by a doting mother. Perhaps as a result, he has a fair dose of narcissism. In this and in his larrikinism, he is similar to former prime minister Bob Hawke, although it is probably true to say that he has been less of a womaniser, and less of a drinker. He gets angry easily, and his natural style is one of high conflict. Julia Gillard, one of his closest friends in politics, told me that she has had quite "ordinary" discussions with him which, to someone passing by, would sound like stand-up rows. "It's a style I feel comfortable with. Not everyone does." Another, less pro-Latham source said: "It is impossible to have a civilised disagreement with him." When Latham – late in life – learned to use email, he used to regularly "flame" people. He had to be taught to think carefully before pressing "send".

He has used abusive language, both in private and in parliament. He is a hater. One former Labor staffer told me Latham used to bring ideas along to policy meetings and "dump them on the table like a cat dumping a dead rat, then storm out if we didn't agree with him". But in recent years, the same man says, he has become better at "bringing people with him. I was surprised to find he has learned how to chair a meeting."

Since becoming leader of the party, Latham has stuck to his promise of "no more crudity". He has shown signs, if not of mellowing, then of discipline.

During his marriage break-up, and at about the same time as he resigned from the frontbench in 1998, Latham clearly went through a wild period – drinking heavily, socialising widely. At this time he must have felt he had "done his dash" – that obscurity on the backbench might be the most he could achieve. This is the period to which much of the gossip about him relates, and also the period in which he came to know his present wife, Janine Lacy. He certainly behaved badly, even cruelly, to Gabrielle Gwyther, while showing all the signs of being in considerable turmoil himself.

Gwyther impressed me, and others who interviewed her, as an essentially honest but angry and hurt woman, although she has remarried. She is nobody's doormat. She is a sociologist; reading her papers on Sydney's "aspirational" suburbs one can see that there must have been considerable cross-fertilisation between her work and that of her husband. In the acknowledgements section of his big book, *Civilising Global Capital*, Latham wrote, "without the support and advice of Gabrielle Latham, all aspects of this project would have been much diminished. In ways that only we might properly understand, this book is as much her achievement as mine." Gwyther seemed to me to have made a determined decision that she would not be written out of history. Thrust into the limelight by her ex-husband's success, she had two options: say nothing and disappear from the narrative, or tell her story as she saw it. She chose the latter. I don't think she ever rang a journalist, but she answered questions willingly when approached. She refused some requests, including one from *Sunday*.

Latham has also been cruel beyond the bounds of necessity to his enemies, including those he vanquished within the Labor Party at Liverpool when he became mayor. He has admitted as much:

> It was a divisive period; I rubbed their noses into it. I suppose that was a mistake at the time. I could've run a more unified, harmonious council, but in the politics – the hotbed municipal politics of the day – it wasn't like that. And one thing I've learned from that period – and probably from in the Parliament here being, at times, too divisive a figure – is to get a better capacity for bringing people together.

Latham's supporters will tell you he has changed in deeper ways than the exigencies of an election campaign could bring about. Diagnosed with testicular cancer in 1994 during his marriage to Gwyther, Latham was once told he was unlikely ever to be a father. Becoming one, and the new stability in his personal life, has mellowed him, his friends claim. Julia Gillard talks about other changes, which are less to do with Latham himself than with success. They are brought about by "the things we do to leaders, like shutting up and listening when they speak". The position itself brings gravitas. There is less need for shouting and scrapping.

One of the most enamoured of his supporters compares Latham to Shakespeare's character Prince Hal in *Henry IV* – the wastrel heir to the throne. Hal knocks around the fleshpots of London with Falstaff and his cronies, and seems incapable of showing due respect to his father, his kingdom, or to anything but his own sense of fun. Everyone fears for what England will suffer under his rule. But power brings greatness. When he ascends to the throne, Prince Hal – now Henry V – banishes Falstaff. When the Dauphin mocks him over his wild youth, he says:

> Tell him he has made a match with such a wrangler that all the courts of France will be disturb'd with chases. And we understand him well. How he comes o'er us with our wilder days, not measuring what use we made of them ... I will keep my state, Be like a king, and show my sail of greatness.

I don't think Latham is Henry V. Perhaps he has a sail of greatness, but I don't think his use of his "wilder days" was calculated.

I also doubt he has the powers of self-examination demonstrated by Shakespeare's Henry V. Gabrielle Gwyther told me Latham had never read a novel in his life. She and others told me of his fascination for the character Kurtz in the film *Apocalypse Now*. Latham is apparently unaware the film is based on a novel – Joseph Conrad's *Heart of Darkness*. As for other cultural figures, Gwyther said Latham did not enjoy the arts, with the exception of the work of Vincent Van Gogh. "Why him?" I asked Gwyther. She laughed: "Perhaps because Van Gogh was mad and cut off his ear." Latham has also studied the life of Jesus Christ, while never professing to be a Christian. It is tempting to draw some conclusions about Latham's character from the cultural icons that have touched him. Kurtz is one of the darkest characters in twentieth-century fiction. Christ personifies courage and virtue. Christ and Kurtz were both leaders. Christ, Kurtz and Van Gogh were martyrs. They were quintessential outsiders. All the things I know about Latham suggest an internal life in high relief, an almost adolescent romantic fascination with good and evil, and a chiaroscuro of the extreme. There is something alarming about this, but also something immature.

I suspect that Latham has been driven most of his life by the fear – perhaps terror is not too strong a word – of failure. For the boy from Green Valley it must always have seemed likely that despite all his cleverness and drive, and despite the fact that he had been anointed by Gough, he would be buried by circumstance and condemned to obscurity and frustration – that all his fine mind and keen ambition would come to nothing. To avoid that end, he has trampled on many people and had scant regard for feelings and reputation. Perhaps he has matured in recent years with the birth of his sons, and grown some wisdom and compassion to match his sharp intelligence. Gough Whitlam has remarked, "He has grown in every job he has held."

Nevertheless in July Mark Latham paid some of the price for his past. It may yet cost him the election. That would be truly Shakespearian.

Surely the most damaging revelations that emerged from the July fever which overtook Canberra do not concern Latham's character, but rather the character of our political culture, and in particular our political journalism. There is nothing wrong with checking out rumours – that is part of a journalist's job. I did it myself. Sitting on the sidelines watching these events unfold and wondering what I would write myself, I could understand the difficulties of deciding, working to a daily deadline, what to reveal and what to keep quiet. Nor is the report card uniformly bad. Some journalists, such as Michelle Grattan of the *Age*, made the obvious checks and decided not to publish the video rumour. Others became, for a few days at least, unusually pretentious gossip columnists.

I object less to the fact that the political journalists spent the best part of a week talking about a story that wasn't, than to the fact that they have neglected so much else – so much of what really matters. Acres of newsprint and hours of screen time have been devoted to Latham's past. Very little has been devoted to his ideas. Latham has been accused of opportunism for emphasising social issues rather than the economy, and for talking "soft" – about babies and reading to children – but these ideas are not being peddled purely for the purposes of the election campaign.

They are part of an intellectual framework and a political architecture that he has been developing for most of his adult life.

As a result, after all the broadcast time and all the newsprint spent on discussing the man, few people realise that he has written five books, and that they are a more reliable guide to what we might be in for than allegations and counter-allegations about what did or did not happen fifteen years ago in Liverpool.

Already the ideas in the books are being reflected in both the policies and strategies of Latham's Labor. This is reason enough for controversy. I wonder whether Latham is frustrated, or relieved, that his books are being so ignored?

LIVERPOOL

Governor Lachlan Macquarie founded Liverpool in 1810 on the rising banks of the Georges River. Its roads and public buildings were built by convicts. Life was never comfortable. The conflicts with the Darug tribe have been described as Australia's first war. From early days, *who* you were in Liverpool was defined largely by *where* you were. Ex-convicts farmed the land along the river flats. The blue-bloods had big grazing properties stretching west to the Nepean River. The settlement of Liverpool was the divider between bush and city, a fringe and frontier town determined by and serving the needs of the centre, while resenting its demands.

Then came the social engineering of the 1960s, and Liverpool was transformed. Green Valley was the largest estate ever to be built by the Housing Commission. Twenty-five thousand people were housed in 6000 new fibro homes, strung out along the rises and falls of the countryside. Liverpool was now one of the fastest growing areas in the country. With its growth its relationship to the centre changed. By the end of the twentieth century, fringe settlements like Liverpool were defining the politics of the country.

No government can hold power without support in the seats on the fringes of the cities. Some say the tail has begun to wag the dog, but given the demographics it would be more accurate to say that the tail *is* the dog. In one of the world's most urban countries, the immediate affairs of the suburbs were always going to demand attention. Impressions to the contrary can only be seen as illusions.

Don and Lorraine Latham were one of the many couples with a young family who moved to Green Valley, drawn by the cheap housing. Among their neighbours were the Conways, including Casey Conway, who was to become a big part of the Mark Latham story. Conway could be seen as Latham's shadow side – what might have been and what he did not want to become. I suspect Conway represents many of Latham's fears. Casey

Conway was a working man, like Latham's father. Like Mark Latham, he was outspoken and aggressive in argument, and a good hater. Like Latham, he has also been a Labor politician and a former Mayor of Liverpool. Casey Conway still lives in the small Green Valley house where he raised his family. The Lathams have moved on. Today Mark lives in Glen Alpine in nearby Campbelltown. Glen Alpine real estate was marketed as "the answer to your dreams" when it was developed by the Lend Lease Corporation in the 1980s. It is aimed at the successful aspirationals. People in Glen Alpine have big houses, and often big mortgages. They've made it up the "ladder of opportunity".

Mark Latham was wrong in July this year when he said it was a Liberal Party dirt unit spreading gossip about his past. I am aware of the origin of the stories about Latham's time at Liverpool, because copies of the same material have been faxed to me. This has been done not by the Liberal Party, but by Casey Conway. When I was in Liverpool in May, Conway was already sending material to Piers Akerman, the *Daily Telegraph* columnist. He had already spoken to Michael Duffy, who was writing a biography of Latham and Tony Abbott. He was already co-ordinating Latham's many other enemies for a media campaign.

Conway had drafted a letter to be signed by himself and five other former mayors and deputy mayors condemning Latham's record as Mayor of Liverpool. This letter was later "revealed" on the Channel Nine *Sunday* program.

I asked Conway whom he planned to vote for in the federal election. He said he couldn't vote Labor. "Labor is run by big business. I have seen the evidence. Look on the Australian Electoral Commission website and you can see all the donations made by big companies." Nor, as an old unionist, could he vote for the Liberal Party. "But the Liberal Party might get a copy of this," he said, indicating the letter.

"It's a strong letter," I remarked.

He grinned. "Well, Latham should have shown more respect. He'll pay for it now."

When Casey Conway's family was young – and when Mark Latham was not yet at school – Conway was rising before daylight each day to make the long train trip into central Sydney for work. He was a plasterer, working for big building companies. Often he was unemployed. He remembers: "Recession, depression, whatever they called it. They had different names for it, but it meant no work." Today he is partially deaf from so many years working next to nail-guns and sanders. On top of the hard work involved in merely staying afloat, Casey Conway became a unionist and an active Labor Party member. He taught himself public speaking and built up confidence at the local Toastmasters Club. He became a councillor, and eventually a Mayor of Liverpool. It isn't hard to imagine how much the achievement must have meant to him. In the mid-1980s, he was one of a group of councillors who contested among themselves for the mayoralty. It was a prize bitterly fought over. Michael Byrne, then active in the East Liverpool Progress Association, remembers that it seemed as though half of each year would be taken up with the battle for the mayoralty, and the following half recovering from the wounds.

For hard-working men who had done everything tough, the mayoralty was a mark of life achievement. The chains and robes of office were worn with chest-swelling pride. Conway was mayor for two years from 1984 and again for twelve months in 1987. By then, another Green Valley resident was beginning to show an interest in local politics. Mark Latham was in his twenties – the same age as Casey Conway's son. He was working for the NSW Labor leader, Bob Carr, and was known to have a special relationship with Liverpool's Labor patriarch, Gough Whitlam.

Michael Byrne remembers meeting Latham when he first began to sit in the public gallery at council meetings. Latham, Byrne says, was "like a tiger watching, summing up the council". The two men soon fell to talking. Byrne was an activist too. In the previous few years he had become one of those driving the area's most influential residents' action group, the East Liverpool Progress Association. The Association had council in its sights. Council was, in Byrne's view, run by "narks, nongs and opportunists", including Labor Party hacks more interested in their own power battles than in the people they served. In 1983, the Association had scored a victory over Labor, getting two of its own candidates elected in the East Ward. In 1987, Latham stood and won back much of the Labor vote. He was lucky to be the candidate. He was not popular with his ALP colleagues and had won preselection by just one vote. He then door-knocked every single household in the ward.

Byrne and Latham could have been rivals, but in fact they soon became friends. Latham went against the dominant Labor faction on council to condemn an unpopular development in the East Ward, and he seemed to be criticising his colleagues most of the time. Byrne liked his style. Byrne was soon telling Progress Association members that Latham "seems to be on about the same things we are on about". If Latham were to become mayor, Byrne thought, the Progress Association could almost retire from the battle. There didn't seem to be much chance of such a thing happening. Mark Latham was already hated by his colleagues, which wasn't surprising given the hard time he gave them. It was impossible to imagine them electing him mayor. The Association, however, had already begun a campaign to have the mayor popularly elected, rather than chosen by the councillors.

A clipping from the *Liverpool Champion* in 1988 gives an idea of the atmosphere. Casey Conway, the Mayor, told the paper that Latham, then twenty-eight, was "arrogant, lacking in wisdom and behaving like a bull at a gate". Latham had ignored the advice of his elders and was wasting too much of the council officers' time by asking questions, Conway said. Latham had asked 190 questions in council meetings since he had been elected. All the other alderman combined had only asked fourteen.

'I have a son his age, and if he behaved like him I'd give him a smack in the mouth," Conway said. "He's got to learn to respect people, he refuses to show humility." Conway objected to Latham foreshadowing proposed reforms to council, including freedom-of-information legislation, workers' participation in decision-making and changes to the rate structure.

Just a few weeks after Conway's remarks, another, less well-publicised clash took place between the two men. It concerned a piece of Latham's personal history – the means by which he had overcome the financial crisis caused by his father's death and been able to continue his education. When Don Latham died, Mark Latham was in his final year of university. He was also the secretary of the local branch of the ALP, having joined the previous year and impressed everyone with his brilliance. Now it seemed he might have to leave university to work and support his mother and sisters. A committee of his fellow members, including a former Deputy Mayor of Liverpool, Frank Heyhoe, decided to help him. Casey Conway still has a copy of the March 1981 letter, authored by the elders of the branch. It reads:

> Dear Casey,
>
> We are writing to you on a very confidential basis, relative to the recent death of Mr Don Latham who, as you know, was the father of our ALP Branch Secretary, Mark Latham. Some of us are concerned that, following Don's death, it is proving very difficult for Mark to continue his University studies, rather than seek employment and provide for his mother and his three younger sisters. Mark is in his final year of the Bachelor of Economics degree, and we know you would agree that it would be tragic if he were forced to miss out on his education.
>
> To assist Mark's family and to ensure that his potential in education is not lost to the Australian Labor Party, a Committee of four has been formed to organise a weekly contribution of $2 a week from each contributing member for an education fund.

There were twenty-five members of the fund. Casey Conway was one of them. The amount of $50 a week was, in combination with Latham's earnings from a bar job, enough to keep him at university. His education was not "lost" to the Labor Party – nor to the nation. Just seven years later, some of those who had organised the whip-around were wishing they hadn't bothered. Having given him the chance to better himself, they had become the main targets of his criticism.

In one of the several fiery council meetings at that time, something was said that led to Latham becoming aware – probably for the first time – that Conway had been one of those whose regular $2 contributions had kept him at university. Conway denies he raised the matter himself, but in one way or another Latham found out about it and was spurred to act. He worked out what he thought the total amount of Conway's contribution would have been, and went to an automatic teller machine to withdraw the amount. It was $400. The first Conway knew of it was when one of Latham's friends thrust the cash in his face. Conway was insulted. He refused the money and suggested it be given to charity. A few days later, Latham sent him a receipt – which Conway still holds – for a donation of $400 to Meals on Wheels.

For Conway, these events are proof of Latham's black soul. Debts of this kind, he says, cannot be redeemed with cash. It is easy to understand why he was insulted.

It is also easy to see the affair from Latham's point of view. Just twenty-eight, angry and in a hurry, he had been confronted by a debt he no longer wished to owe. He felt as though he had been "bought", and he wanted to buy himself back. He wanted to be free from obligations. Yet he would not, or could not, pay in the only currency that might have meant something. He would not give what Conway really wanted – a little respect.

Latham was by now regularly telling the local newspapers that the council was old-fashioned. Its day had passed, he said. He addressed the local chamber of commerce and said that the missing ingredient for the last three decades at council had been leadership. Latham was writing position papers and proposals for economic development. Michael Byrne remembers visiting him at his house and seeing the dining-room table always covered with papers and research. Little of what he advocated was welcome.

The East Liverpool Progress Association, meanwhile, had succeeded against Labor Party opposition in forcing a popular election for the mayoralty. When the election was held in 1991, Latham was not the Labor Party's first choice of candidate. That was Alderman Pat Pantaleo. Latham was one of his supporters, but Pantaleo was forced to stand aside after the East Liverpool Progress Association exposed him in a breach of the *Local Government Act* over a failure to declare a conflict of interest. Even then, Latham was not his party's favourite. He was chosen at least partly because the East Liverpool Progress Association told the party that it would throw its preferences behind Latham, and only Latham – not any other Labor Party candidate. Byrne still remembers the venom of the phone calls he took from other Labor Party members.

In September 1991, Mark Latham, then just thirty years old, swept to power elected for four years. He had scored 45.4 per cent of the primary votes and 62 per cent after preferences had been distributed. His nearest rival was Alderman Colin Harrington, an independent and the incumbent. He received just 14.7 per cent of the primary vote. Harrington, along with Latham's Labor colleagues, was to become another enemy. Latham had come to office owing very few favours, and almost in spite of the efforts of the party he represented.

In an interview to mark his taking up the office, the local paper asked Latham why he was so hated. Did he lack personal skills? Latham replied, "I probably don't think enough about what other people are thinking. I don't sometimes appreciate that by doing something logical, other people are building within themselves animosities and fears. I've got to think about the way people respond to things that I say and do."

Meanwhile Latham took to referring to his predecessors, and many of the serving councillors, as "crooks and dunces". Under Latham, the council was effectively run by himself and two other relatively young supporters: Councillors Alex Sanchez and Craig Knowles (now the New South Wales Minister for Planning). Already Latham was being spoken of as a possible future prime minister. There was speculation he would challenge the sitting federal member, John Kerin, for preselection. Sanchez and Knowles were his heirs-apparent on council.

Having won power, Latham set about using it. He quit his job with Bob Carr to devote himself full-time to his mayoral duties, taking a cut in pay to do so. Over the next few months, he scrapped mentions of God in the prayer that opened each council meeting. He had the Union Jack removed from the city's flag, and the Queen's picture removed from the council chamber. The city needed a more mature, multicultural and independent identity, he said. For Casey Conway and his cohorts, perhaps the most galling thing of all was that within a few days Latham had announced that the mayoral robes and chain, the marks of office that had been so coveted, would be sent to the museum. They were no longer relevant to the '90s, Latham said. Young people laughed at them. They had made the people who wore them look ridiculous.

It is not hard to see why Casey Conway and his fellow former mayors hate Mark Latham, and it is easy to sympathise with them. They were men who against the odds had given their time and service to the city, only to be rubbished and usurped by a man young enough to be their son.

And yet, talking to Conway, there is also the inescapable conclusion that Latham was probably right to oppose them. Conway is ready to attack Latham's financial record, and has been working hard to circulate figures suggesting his management of council was a mess. But when I asked him for the financial records to back his claims, it became clear that he was working from information provided by others. Nor could he tell me the details of how and when the financial problems had emerged. He confessed he couldn't read a balance sheet. Unlike Latham, he had never had the opportunity for a decent education.

It was during his period as a councillor, but before he was elected mayor, that Latham wrote his first book. A slim volume, titled *Reviving Labor's Agenda*, it was published in 1990 – six years before the Howard government defeated Keating largely thanks to the swing of western Sydney voters away from Labor. Latham was prophetic. He wrote that "themes of Labor neglect" were beginning to emerge in the suburbs, which had until recently returned Labor members. "Conservatives are using this to question the legitimacy of Labor Governments."

Latham argued that local issues and local government were the key to reinvigorating Labor. People had given up on the idea that government could improve their lives. They were remote from the process of democracy — spectators, rather than participants. Reform parties must find new ways to connect with the public. The political system gave undue power to the articulate and to sectional interests:

> It is improper to assume that every person has equal access to government. In a complex democracy where power is centralised, only the privileged few can resemble Rousseau's ideal citizen "ever ready to fly to the public assembly".

Latham wrote that the decline in unionism had undermined the Labor Party's traditional legitimacy and its claim to be broadly based. It must seek new constituencies, and become a community-based party with an emphasis on local issues and new forums for public participation in government.

His experience with local government had led him to question the federal system. If one was building the nation from scratch, he said, one would not include the states. Instead, federal government would regulate and fund services delivered at local and regional level. He wrote that the founding arguments for federalism in 1901, concerning differences and rivalries between the colonies, now looked absurd. Australia was a relatively uniform nation; any real differences could be found at local — not state — level. Australia's federal system was one of the main barriers to effective government and reform. Bureaucracies were created that had nothing to do but monitor the delivery of services by other bureaucracies. Federal government raised 80 per cent of public revenue, but the bulk of services were provided by state and local governments. Latham accepted that the states could not be abolished, but argued that the Hawke government had an historic opportunity. With Labor in power in five states, it should be possible to achieve lasting change in health and education without changing the constitution. But the Hawke government showed no sign of taking up the challenge.

Latham's first book was the first articulation of the recurring themes of his political career. *Reviving Labor's Agenda* contained in embryonic form most of the ideas he was later to develop in his big book, *Civilising Global Capital*, and which today are beginning to drive Labor Party policy. Already he saw the political world in terms of an "insider–outsider" split. Already he was questioning the federal system and thinking in resolutely local terms about the "management of place".

Latham used Liverpool City Council as his exemplar in *Reviving Labor's Agenda*. Under his influence, the council had copied an idea of "precinct committees", first pioneered by Ted Mack, the independent mayor of North Sydney Council. Liverpool established precinct committees for each area and they held regular public meetings. Latham wrote:

> The great virtue of the precinct committees is their ability to bring local government within reach of all residents. All manner of municipal issues can be addressed at these informal meetings each month in each suburb. Precincts are the kind of initiative that provides an equality of opportunity for all to participate in the decisions that affect the style and quality of suburban life.

This sort of democracy, he said, would lead to a more tolerant society. Civic abilities would be developed. "People learn that their own interests are served best, not at the expense of others, but by cooperating in activities which only the community can organise."

Look through the local papers from Latham's period as mayor, and one can sense the ferment. In his first few weeks he presented a mayoral minute to council, fifty pages in length, outlining his vision for the city as a centre of regional development. He wanted Liverpool to be a "lifestyle council" with an emphasis on equality of opportunity. He wanted the children of the area to have the same opportunities as the "insiders" of the inner suburbs.

> Our vision for Liverpool is based on what social democrats and socialists have been trying to achieve for centuries – giving the next generation better opportunities and chances in life than our generation. I want children growing up in suburbs like Hammondville, Holdsworthy, Warwick Farm, Lurnea and Green Valley to benefit from good books in good libraries, learning and culture in the Powerhouse [Museum], [to] study music in the comfort of the Green Valley Music Centre, train in quality recreation centres and heated pools, and find good care and tuition in our child-care centres.

Latham's council began unprecedented spending on public works, partly financed by the sale of part of a public road to Westfield Shopping Town. There was to be a ring-road system to reduce traffic in the city centre, and a new pedestrian mall in the main street. Council budgeted to build a heated pool complex at the Whitlam Recreation Centre at a cost of $4.8 million, and to upgrade the area's main park around Chipping Norton Lakes – created long ago by sand-mining. The Casula Powerhouse regional arts centre was to be upgraded. Council offered local businesses guidance to introduce Total Quality Management programs. On a micro level, a backlog of maintenance work on roads, buildings and drains was to be addressed. Works of art were commissioned for the city streets, and the CBD was to be "cleaned up" with incentives for businesses that lent a hand. Liverpudlians, Latham said, should be proud of their city. He told the local paper that one of his main aims was to lift the community's civic pride, including their expectations of their elected representatives. He wanted to convince people that government could, and should, make a difference to their lives. Latham was available to talk personally to residents at regular, advertised intervals. Councillors and staff were instructed to attend the precinct committee meetings.

The mall became one of the signature battles of Latham's period as mayor. It was opposed by the local chamber of commerce, but a 1991 referendum showed that the population as a whole backed the idea. Vitriolic public meetings with traders dominated the headlines for weeks. Latham had no time for courting business if he saw it opposing positive change.

Meanwhile he was using his position to make his mark on state and federal politics. He fought the state government over the toll on the M5 freeway, and – in a move that might yet embarrass him – supported the siting of Sydney's second airport at Badgery's Creek, because of the jobs it might bring to Liverpool. Latham was soon using his position on the Western Sydney Regional Organisation of Councils as a platform. Here, too, he made enemies and infuriated his state Labor colleagues. He made headlines in the metropolitan daily newspapers by advocating the closing of small, inner-Sydney hospitals so services could be moved to needy areas in the west.

In August 1992 – nearly one year into Latham's term as mayor – the general manager of Liverpool City Council, David Mead, resigned. The local paper reported that Mead had left because he couldn't work with Latham. The two men were said not to be on speaking terms. Mead took a new job as general manager of Baulkham Hills Council, one of the wealthy enclaves of Sydney's western suburbs; over the next few years, he took it from near bankruptcy to a healthy financial position. He is, others in local government suggest, a conscientious, competent but conservative manager. In Latham's view, his conservatism was a fatal flaw. Liverpool was growing at a phenomenal rate. Bold new strategies were needed if the generations of the future were to be better provided for than the past residents of Green Valley had been. (Mead has declined to speak to the many journalists, including me, who have approached him in the last few months.)

Latham went headhunting for a new general manager. It was known within New South Wales local government circles that he did not want a traditional "town clerk". Instead he hired John Walker from Perth, a man with experience in both private industry and local government, and a record of managing organisational change.

Even without Mark Latham, the early 1990s was a period of great change in local government in Australia, particularly New South Wales. A new *Local Government Act* was proclaimed in 1993, and its likely contents were already known when Latham became mayor in late 1991. The new law gave councils much greater independence from state government control, but also placed heavy emphasis on public accountability and efficiency.

At the same time, the ethos of economic rationalism was sweeping all tiers of government. At the local level, the latest thing was competitive tendering – putting council services out for tender, rather than employing a large "outdoor" staff. Latham was an enthusiast for such an approach. In his book *Reviving Labor's Agenda*, he had written that overseas evidence showed councils could cut costs significantly by reforming along market lines.

Now he was trying to push through a purchaser/provider split of council's functions. Purchasing units would put council services out to tender. Council staff could compete for the business, but so too could outside organisations. It was an idea that was radical at the time, though later it would become a commonplace. Jeff Kennett made competitive tendering compulsory for Victorian local government when he became premier a short while later. Under Latham, Liverpool was to be a pioneer – on the bleeding edge of reform.

Yet Latham had so far failed to convince council's staff of the need for change. They had already passed a unanimous vote of no confidence in his management. They were accusing him of being anti-Labor, and Latham had scarcely placated them by telling the local paper:

> There is nothing in the Labor tradition nor will there ever be which
> calls on elected representatives to cover up for people who blatantly
> abuse the system and the goodwill of the public purse.

He made reference to council staff being paid for falling asleep under trees. The whole system, he implied, was a rort.

Now Walker took on the brief of Latham's reforms with missionary zeal.

Latham's period as Mayor of Liverpool City Council is the only time he has ever run anything. Naturally it has been the focus of attention during the election campaign. Allegations have gone back and forth about the figures – whether Latham's management of council was financially responsible. Peter Costello has publicly urged journalists to investigate. "If you can't run a council, you can't run the country," he has said.

There have been attacks in parliament, and media questioning on the detail. Latham says he was a good economic manager, leaving council in surplus and with a plan to retire all debt. His enemies say he left it with a financial black hole. Piers Akerman was one of the first on the attack. In late July, a commission of inquiry into Liverpool City Council and the Oasis scandal found that in the mid-1990s – after Latham had left – the council had had a $15.4 million deficit in working capital, and that this was the result of decisions made during Latham's time.

None of these allegations has really built up a head of steam, and there are good reasons why. The real scandal may well be that it is almost impossible to tell, with confidence, what the real financial figures are. As anyone who deals regularly with local government accounts knows, this is not a problem confined to Liverpool. Even columns of figures, it seems, can lie, or at least be made to serve whatever purpose is required. Like all "facts" they are refracted through prisms that are to do with values and world-view. In this case, enough ambiguity and uncertainty exists to allow both sides to argue their case with mixed credibility.

Both Latham and his critics have been selective – at best – in their use of figures.

The financial picture forms part of a bigger and even more significant story, which is to do with the possibility and management of radical change. Change is the theme of Latham's political life, as it was for Whitlam before him. The underlying question is whether it is possible, in Australia, to succeed as a radical reformer. A related question suggests itself: what might such success require?

Happily for future historians, there is a source of independent information on how Latham and Walker managed change at Liverpool City Council. In mid-1995, Liverpool was voted one of the top two "reformist" councils in New South Wales in a survey of local government general managers. This brought it to the attention of Dr Robert Jones, an academic specialist on organisational change in local government. Over the next year, Jones conducted hours of tape-recorded interviews with Walker and other council staff. He did not talk to Latham, who had left the mayoralty by the time he began his research, but he was allowed unfettered access to staff and senior management. Jones saw Liverpool as an example of radical change introduced with a sense of urgency. He compared it to other councils where reform had been more gradual.

Walker himself was amazingly frank. He told Jones how ruthless he had been with senior management in his first days. Nine out of twelve people had been "forced or encouraged" to resign. Meanwhile he searched out "right-thinking activists" – the smartest younger people in the organisation. Staff were psychologically and intellectually tested and profiled, and seven were selected to form a fast-track management team. Walker told Jones they were "my messengers – young bright leaders". They "walked the talk" with a "missionary zeal", but they were also Walker's spies. "They were my eyes and ears as well," he told Jones. "The first book I got out of the library when I joined Liverpool City Council was Machiavelli's *The Prince*. It's got a lot to teach about changing culture."

Jones concluded that Walker was not a man for detail. Walker made it clear that he did not intend to stay longer than the term of his contract – four years. He confessed in an interview that he saw his main mission as being to "establish the principles, build the mindset and worry about the details later". Walker spent weeks of his time with council's outdoor staff – the garbage collectors, the men who fixed the potholes in the roads – trying to heal the rift between them and Latham. He regarded the outdoor staff as salt of the earth. It was bad management that was to blame for council's problems, in his view. Walker succeeded where Latham had failed in negotiating an enterprise agreement.

Once Latham had appointed Walker, he stepped back from the day-to-day management of council. Walker said, "[Latham] very clearly outlined to me what council policy was, and my role was to deliver on it. And I delivered on it. And he never once interfered. He didn't come into my day-to-day management." Latham's role, as Walker saw it, was to provide the political support for change. He "kept council away" from Walker. Walker said: "I was the implementer and he was the designer. He was the philosophical driver, the strategist, the policy maker and he should claim credit for most of the things that actually hit the ground. I do claim credit for the capacity to implement, or more accurately, to interpret the policy and find a way to deliver. I didn't just do what I was told. I found the way to deliver the agenda that worked."

Mark Latham had been spoken of as a possible future prime minister since his earliest days on council. In 1993, his chance to enter federal politics came. John Kerin, the member for Werriwa, retired and made it clear that Latham was his chosen successor. In a by-election in February 1994, Latham won the seat despite a 6.2 per cent swing against Labor. He remained Mayor of Liverpool as well, determined to see out his term, but it was not to be. Just a few months later, rumours began to race around council that Latham was sick. He confirmed that he had been diagnosed with testicular cancer. "My first thought was that I was going to die," he confessed recently. But the cancer had been caught early, thanks in part to Latham seeing a program on ABC television that had led him to recognise his symptoms and seek medical advice. (At his community forums, Latham has used this anecdote to assure audiences that he will support and adequately fund the ABC.) After he underwent an operation to remove the diseased testicle, his prognosis was good. Nevertheless, the doctors advised him to reduce his workload. Latham decided to resign from council.

Latham's natural successor was his supporter Alex Sanchez, but the local Labor Party had different ideas. George Paciullo, a former state government minister as well as former mayor, contested the preselection and won it after a ballot plagued with the branch-stacking allegations that were an almost routine feature of Liverpool Labor politics. Paciullo admitted 500 members had been registered just before the ballot, but said these people had simply wanted to demonstrate to him how much he was wanted.

Walker was soon frustrated by the new regime. Shortly after Latham's departure, problems were identified with the implementation of the reform agenda. There were overlaps and gaps between business units, and a lack of accountability. Walker had commissioned an independent organisational review and presented the resulting three-volume report to council. They sat on it for six months, clearly suspicious of Walker and the Latham agenda. Meanwhile senior management positions became vacant, and the new council embarked on its own capital-spending regime – at a time when Walker and Latham had planned to peg back.

Today Walker says Latham and he had always known they were spending up to the limit, and were happy to do so. Liverpool was growing fast. Developers' contributions and rates would flow in to help repay the debt. They made a conscious decision to build the capital works and to tackle the maintenance backlog. They had planned, then, to reign in spending and make council debt-free.

Now problems were emerging. From Walker's point of view, the answer was to push on with the reforms, implementing the purchaser/provider split more completely, and pushing for greater efficiency. The new council did not agree. They wanted to wind back the reform agenda. By 1995, it was clear to Walker that he and the new council could not work together. He allowed himself to be headhunted by the Westpac bank, where he went on to introduce another radical program of organisational change.

Meanwhile Dr Jones returned to Liverpool City Council to interview the new general manager, Brian Carr, and to assess the legacy of the Walker and Latham period. Carr told Jones in their first interview that "the inquests had started" about whether Walker's change program had really been successful. "When you look under the carpet, it's an absolute bloody mess." He suggested to Jones that Liverpool had been a local government laboratory for the idea of the purchaser/provider split, and that most general managers were now saying, "I'm not going to touch that with a bargepole."

Brian Carr said that the detail of the Latham-Walker reforms had never been properly implemented. The purchaser/provider split was more theory than reality. In some areas it hadn't been introduced at all. Where council work had been contracted out, there had been many problems. How often do toilet blocks need to be cleaned? When do the bulbs have to be planted in the gardens? This was the kind of expertise that lived only in the minds of council staff. Encapsulating it in contracts and specifications was not easy. Liverpool had written many of its contracts with specifications that related to how often work should be done, rather than to what standard, and had ended paying extra to have the work done properly. Anticipated savings had not eventuated, and there had been massive duplication, with council staff sometimes sitting idle while private contractors did their work.

Most damaging of all, Brian Carr told Jones that the Latham-Walker regime had left council with a poor financial legacy. It was in Carr's April 1997 interview with Jones that the working capital deficit — $15.5 million, Carr said — was first mentioned. (Working capital is the amount of money left over after current liabilities are taken away from current assets. It is, effectively, the amount of money council has to do things with, after meeting its commitments.) It is this figure that is now being used to question Latham's capacity as a financial manager.

Context is important in assessing the figures for Liverpool City Council. Latham and Walker's successors, Carr and Paciullo, did not run the council well. Both of them are now in disgrace, and the council was sacked as a result of the Oasis affair – an extraordinary saga in which council paid large amounts of money over to private industry to build a football stadium. As the report of the inquiry into the affair, released in late July 2004, makes clear, it is a story of extraordinary incompetence on the part of both Paciullo and Carr, who allowed a "dream" of a sporting stadium to overwhelm proper process and the most basic financial prudence. Sections of the Local Government Act were breached, Carr became a "spin doctor" with a "fetish for secrecy", the councillors were supine and Paciullo acted well beyond his competence. The report of the inquiry has been referred to the Australian Securities and Investment Commission to investigate whether charges should be laid against some of the corporate figures involved.

The Oasis affair could – and should – be the topic of a book by itself, involving as it does a stellar cast of Sydney characters, predatory developers and greedy banks. The result was a cost to council of at least $22 million, with only a concrete slab and a car park to show for it. Liverpool residents will be living with the results, including a lack of money for other, needed, infrastructure, for years.

For this story, it is important to know that many of those who now accuse Latham have themselves had findings made against them. Even council's auditor, PricewaterhouseCoopers, came out with a mixed scorecard, with findings that it had not adequately warned council about the risks of entering into the various commercial agreements.

It was in the auditor's evidence before the inquiry earlier this year that Carr's claim about the $15.5 million deficit got another run. Denis Banicevic of PricewaterhouseCoopers gave a slightly different figure –

$15.9 million – and said it had been caused because the savings from the purchaser/provider split introduced by Latham and Walker had not eventuated. He said council had been placed on a Local Government Department watch list because of concerns about its financial performance. At the inquiry, Carr, Pacullio and Banicevic suggested the deficit, and council's present problems, were in part the legacy of Latham's governance. Because of the deficit, they had been unwilling to finance infrastructure from council's own resources. That was why they had turned to private partners to build their stadium.

Banicevic's evidence was leapt on by Casey Conway, who was sitting in the public gallery at the hearings, and also by Piers Akerman. It was referred to in parliament, which led Latham to defend his economic record.

On 1 June 2004, Latham told parliament that during his time as mayor, council's debt-servicing ratio (the percentage of loan repayments to gross income) had fallen from 17 per cent to 10 per cent, which was half of the Western Sydney average of 20 per cent. He said that in his last budget in 1994, council had adopted a debt-retirement strategy that, if followed, would have made it debt-free in 2005. He said that between 1991 and 1994, council's working funds balance increased from $770,000 to $1.1 million, and that at the end of 1994 – the year in which he left council – the budget surplus was $1.6 million.

In the days following Latham's statement, Councillor Colin Harrington – the man Latham had defeated in the 1991 election for mayor, and also one of the "whistleblowers" who had helped to uncover the Oasis scandal – approached the council's present financial staff to check Latham's figures. Harringon sent the results of this work to Piers Akerman. A copy was given to me and other journalists by Casey Conway.

The results were not good for Latham, who had clearly been deceptively selective in his use of figures. Council staff agreed that the debt-servicing ratio had fallen during Latham's time, but disputed his figures on the Western Sydney average. It was not 20 per cent, but 12.11 per cent.

The staff could find no reference to the debt-retirement strategy Latham claimed to have implemented, other than a mention in the preamble to the 1994–95 budget. All this assessment was complicated by the fact that there had been several changes in local government accounting standards over the relevant period.

Most crucially, the figures for the working fund that Latham had given were also deceptive. These figures were drawn from the budget, not from the clearly more appropriate and reliable audited financial statements. The financial statements for 1994 showed that the working fund had not been $1.1 million, as claimed by Latham. That had been the budgeted figure. The actual figure was a $2.73 million deficit. Latham had left halfway through this year.

Clearly something went seriously wrong with the budget planning. Dr Jones' research makes it clear that the problems were almost certainly in the implementation of the purchaser/provider split, and the real-life difficulties of writing contracts. The problems lay in the fine management of innovation and reform.

But Latham's critics have been misleading as well. The much-quoted $15.5 million deficit in working capital did not emerge in council's accounts until long after Latham had left. Its only mention in an official document is to be found in Brian Carr's preamble to his first annual report in 1997, where he wrote, with nice ambiguity:

> At one stage council's working capital deficit blew out to $15.4 million. However, since then council has cut its deficit to $7.8 million and adopted a strategy to achieve a surplus by 2000.

Nothing indicates when the blow-out occurred, and no figure appears in any of the published financial statements to support the $15.5 million figure. The reason, council staff tell me, is that "carry-overs" – capital works committed to but not yet performed – were not included in the financial accounts by Carr in 1997, and this made the figures appear healthier. It was an unusual move from an accounting point of view.

Carr was happy to give the bad news in his verbal report, but did not make sure the published figures reflected it. Whatever the intention, this had the effect of obscuring when the $15.5 million deficit actually emerged. NSW Department of Local Government figures suggest that it was in 1995–96, after Latham had departed.

Latham's critics say that the deficit figure is nevertheless the legacy of his time as mayor. The efficiencies he budgeted for were meant to pay for the ongoing costs of maintaining and running the new facilities he had built – but the efficiencies never eventuated.

Latham has said in parliament that the problem was rather that the new council did not pursue the reform process. Instead it frustrated, then wound back, the commercialisation and contracting out of council work. At the same time, the new council had overturned decisions to cap future capital works. "In fact, the council in 1996 ran a capital works budget of $35 million and also allowed recurrent costs to escalate. In areas not connected with capital works, operating costs increased by between 32 per cent and 600 per cent. The council lost its cost-control discipline and efficiency dividend."

So what can be said about Latham's period at Liverpool City Council? Very little, with certainty, about the figures in isolation. Clearly there is a discrepancy between the results Latham and Walker budgeted on, and what they actually achieved. Clearly there were problems during Latham's time at council, and these problems were part of the reason – but not the whole or the main reason – for council's fragile condition in the mid-1990s.

Today John Walker remains a Latham fan and a personal friend. He is also a councillor himself, and a member of the Liberal Party. He told me: "I will be working very hard for the return of a Howard Liberal government, but if Mark Latham wins office, I will be very happy. The country will be in good hands." If only the council had pushed on in the direction he and Latham had initiated, he says, all would have been well.

Dr Jones came to the conclusion that if anything, Walker had let Latham down in his management of the purchaser/provider split. John Walker was the first to emphasise that Latham did not intervene in day-to-day management. Partly, Dr Jones believes, the problems arose because Liverpool was a pioneer. Other councils learned from their experience, particularly about the importance of carefully writing contracts.

Nevertheless, Latham and his supporters were responsible for what the council was doing. They were caught up in the desire to be cutting-edge reformers. It is clear from Jones' research that Latham prevented Walker from being frustrated, impeded or even significantly questioned by hostile councillors. The bundle of urges generally labelled economic rationalism were in their heyday, and Latham was a convert. By the end of the 1990s, many councils that had experimented with competitive tendering had wound it back. Purchaser/provider splits are still controversial, but experience suggests they are often simply too hard to manage in practice.

How do we assess the record of success of a government? Surely, in part, by its legacy – what survives after the leaders have gone. When Gough Whitlam worked with Mark Latham on the book about the Whitlam years, he was able to point to institutions and attitudes that survived his sacking. Most notably, there was Medibank, and a generation of university graduates who owed their education to his reforms. There was also an altered understanding of the responsibilities of federal government.

What is the legacy of Latham's time at Liverpool City Council? Michael Byrne, the man who helped bring him to power, acknowledges that it doesn't look good at first glance. Ten years after the Latham years, council has been sacked in disgrace. Byrne comments: "With the political pillar collapsed, it didn't take long for the administrative moves to fall. On the surface Mark's legacy is a swag of malcontents." The problem, Byrne says, is that Latham was only there for two and a half years, and his successors were not of his calibre and were hostile to what he had achieved.

Nor did Latham's fine ideas on citizen democracy survive him. Within months of his departure, the precinct committees were collapsing. The inquiry this year found that far from having high levels of citizen involvement, Liverpool City Council was extraordinarily secretive and defensive.

Some things remain from Latham's two and a half years as mayor. Today it is hard to imagine Liverpool without the capital works Latham built. The mall he pushed through against such opposition is now an acknowledged success, and the heart of the city. The other resources he provided are part of what makes Liverpool liveable.

At both a symbolic and a practical level, the arc of Latham's Liverpool City Council – massive social change, huge infrastructure projects, a re-invigoration of the population, followed by a fall into chaos and financial disarray, confusion and counter-claim – follows a little too neatly that of the Whitlam federal government. The story even ends with the leader's premature departure, and later with the sacking of a government, though not that of Mark Latham.

Introducing and managing radical change is never easy. It is hard to think of an Australian political leader who has done it and been acknowledged as a success. If I had been granted an interview with Mark Latham, one of the questions would have been what he had learned, at Liverpool, about change.

I would worry if the answer were "nothing".

The ground keeps shifting under my feet. I had written a section of this essay predicting, on the basis of Latham's books, that he would use the possibility of coast-to-coast Labor governments to promise a new era of co-operation between the states and the Commonwealth on health and education. No sooner had I written this than, on 15 July, Latham and the state premiers did the very thing I had anticipated. They signed an agreement and promised an end to cost- and blame-shifting in health, education, housing and indigenous affairs, and a new emphasis on uniform national standards. I claim no special powers of prescience. It is all there in the books. Although the agreement was interpreted in the media as a political move to counter the Howard government's scare campaign about the risks of nation-wide Labor governments, as with so much else that has happened during the campaign, the roots go deep in Latham's history. In his very first book, Latham lamented that Bob Hawke was not using the historic opportunity of having Labor in power federally and in five states. Latham has made it clear that he plans to act where Hawke did not.

As I write this, the majority of Labor's policies have yet to be announced. The press gallery has been baying for their release, in between interviewing Gabrielle Gwyther, interviewing each other to establish whether or not a Liberal Party dirt unit exists, and chasing non-existent buck's night videos. In particular, the media have called for the release of Labor's taxation, health and welfare policies. Here Latham has promised much – lower taxation, an improved health insurance rebate and greater income security – but without any accompanying detail.

Dare I make predictions, given the certainty that by the time this reaches its readers, the ground will have shifted again? If Latham's written work proves a reliable guide to his intentions in government, then we may be in for a roller-coaster ride of change. He has always been in politics to make a difference. Perhaps the experience at Liverpool, the mellowing of age and the exigencies of the party room and of politics will have altered his thrust. Certainly some of the suggestions in his books have the potential to seriously scare the electorate. Perhaps he will go slowly and carefully – but I doubt it. Latham has held terrier-like to some central ideas throughout his career. I don't think this has altered. I think the signs so far suggest that the Latham of the books is the same man now struggling to become prime minister.

He wrote in his most recent book, From the Suburbs:

> No one ever expects the Coalition to do much – they just preside, preen themselves and put the country to sleep. The weight is always on Labor to do things.

Watching the election campaign proceed with Latham's books at my side has been bizarre, almost funny and certainly tragic. The man who laments, in Civilising Global Capital, the way in which television has eroded civil society has now visited the set of Big Brother and even claimed to be a regular viewer. It's sad, but not surprising. In Australian public life there aren't many ways to talk about ideas, other than to deride them. The way the game is played means that Latham the politician must play down Latham the thinker. Many people I have spoken to don't know that Latham has written books. When these are referred to in the media – which is not often – it is invariably in negative terms. Latham has been, we are told, a "policy wonk". The journalist and commentator Greg Sheridan has said that despite his books, "You'd be hard put to know what ideas Latham stood for." Sheridan claimed Latham's ideas had "been numerous, flighty, contradictory, often as [Kevin] Rudd once put it 'just plain wacky'." Other journalists have also relayed the impression that Latham's claim to being a thinker is in some way suspect. All this has been done with barely any discussion of the ideas themselves.

Greg Sheridan's analysis of Latham's work is plainly wrong. For better or worse, Latham's ideas have been remarkably consistent and clearly stated. It is not true that his intellectual record is flighty or contradictory.

The "contradictions" are either non-existent, or else fully acknowledged developments in his thought. Latham's ideas may be radical, but they are hardly "wacky". His books show a penetrating, analytical mind. He could have been an academic: a sociologist like his former wife, or a political scientist. As the sociologist David Burchell has stated:

> The idea of Latham's intellectual "flakiness" wasn't invented by the press gallery. It was first cultivated by Latham's late opponents in the Labor Party, who dripped it into the ears of the press gallery with all the cloak-and-dagger of Shakespearian stage-murderers. Messrs Abbott and Costello reinforced it, with slapstick. And it was cemented by means of that longstanding convention in Australian public life that says that anyone who pretends to read books (let alone write one) is a poseur. It's that old Australian schoolboy's terror of being taken for the schoolroom "conch", only taken to the next level.

It is true that there are big, possibly fatal gaps in Latham's thinking. He has had little or nothing to say on foreign affairs, other than vague and hopeful statements that a more civic-minded society will in turn be more tolerant and trusting of foreigners and international institutions. He has had almost nothing to say about the environment, except as it relates to urban living. He has had nothing to say about the arts, other than as a sub-branch of education. Latham is an analytical thinker, not an abstract one. He has not strayed into areas where he has no direct experience.

Senator Bob Brown told me that he got the impression Latham had never really thought about the environment. His responses on the day that Brown showed him around the old-growth forests of Tasmania in March 2004 were so bald as to be comical, particularly when placed alongside Brown's reverence. When asked about the majestic Gandalf Staff tree, Latham said, "It's a big tree." When asked about the even more impressive Cave Tree, he said it was a big tree with a hole in it. "He just wasn't giving anything," says Brown. It isn't true that Latham has Bob Brown's endorsement. That impression was created through bad media reporting.

Yes, Brown described him as the next prime minister of Australia – "That is just fact. Who else is there?" – but he also chided and challenged him for saying, on the previous day, that logging in Tasmanian old-growth forests would be allowed to continue. The Labor Party promised to ratify the Kyoto Treaty before Latham was leader. Since he assumed the leadership, Labor's main environmental initiatives have been to promise a ban on plastic bags and to co-opt Peter Garrett. Brown says Latham is well aware that the environment is an important issue, particularly for young voters. "On the other hand, he ran into the Tasmanian Labor Party, and they are small-minded, nasty and thuggish." Although Brown doesn't say it, Latham needs the goodwill of the states to do the other things – the things on which he *has* written, and *has* got a point of view.

During the campaign so far, Latham has seemed to me to be trying to give his ideas tangible form – books for kids as a concrete example of the importance of education, and community forums as a concrete example of the kind of civic connectedness he advocates. The policies that have been announced show, I think, that Latham's ideas as expressed in his books may well be a reliable guide to what he will try to do. I think that to the extent that journalists have failed to engage with Latham's ideas, they have failed the electorate. To the extent that Latham has given up on communicating his ideas, he has succumbed to the toxic climate of public life, or perhaps merely backed away from presenting them in a context where they will be seriously challenged.

It is hard to imagine that all of Latham's ideas will translate into policy. Some are surely too radical to be politically sellable. And yet any assessment of the man and what he might mean cannot be complete without summarising the program of social change he has outlined.

Latham's "big book" was *Civilising Global Capital*, published in 1998 by Allen & Unwin. With the sub-title "New Thinking for Labor", it had its origins in federal Labor's heavy defeat in 1996, and was a summary and an historical analysis of the policy dilemmas facing the party, together with suggestions for ways forward. Latham argued that the defeat of

Keating was a signal from the electorate that Labor needed to reassess its policies and values from first principles. This, he said, was a challenge faced by social-democratic parties the world over, brought on by the end of the post-war certainties of the welfare state, and the impact of foot-loose global capital. Since *Civilising Global Capital*, Latham's books and articles have been shorter, easier to read and more vigorous in expression. Often they are based on his speeches. Sometimes, such as with *What Did You Learn Today?* – his 2001 book on education – they contain further development of his ideas, but mostly they offer digestible, easily com-municated versions of the proposals in *Civilising Global Capital*. Having written the "big book" and seen it either ignored or derided, Latham seems to have set about trying to make it communicable, politically palat-able, and even compelling.

As already noted, several big ideas recur throughout his writing, and these underpin the specific proposals. Central is the notion of insiders and outsiders, two groups with unequal access to information and influ-ence. Following from this, as Latham writes in *What Did You Learn Today?*:

> Most of the equity issues facing society are now positioned around two factors: education and geography … postcodes have become a reliable guide to socio-economic outcomes. The new dividing line is being drawn between information-rich and information-poor neighbourhoods, no matter whether they are located in metropol-itan or non-metropolitan areas.

The paradox of globalisation, he argues, is that when economies become international in their orientation, economic disadvantage becomes increasingly local.

The most striking part of *Civilising Global Capital* is a section entitled "Managing the Commons", in which Latham uses the metaphor of the old European system of the village common to represent the demands on the modern state. The social-democratic project is "groaning", he says, under ever-increasing demands placed upon it in the name of equity.

The commons are no longer sustainable. The idea of the welfare state has
to be rethought.

On a piece of common land, everyone has unrestricted grazing rights.
If someone limits their grazing, only they suffer. Latham writes:

> The system virtually forces everyone to draw as much as possible on
> the resource, even though it is limited and only slowly renewable
> ... The practice of social justice has no clearer moral purpose than
> to act diligently as custodians of the commons.

This means guarding against the overloading of government. Since the
Second World War, Latham says, well-meaning reformers, particularly
those from the Left, have loaded new functions onto government beyond
its carrying capacity. In consequence, the modern welfare state has become
dysfunctional. Big, centralised bureaucracies – such as Centrelink and
Medicare – have deprived people of direct control over, and knowledge of,
the use of "the commons". In the absence of such knowledge, people who
work hard and pay their taxes come to resent welfare recipients. Insecurity
caused by globalisation has reversed the tall poppy syndrome:

> In so much of the public arena – talkback radio, tabloid TV, the
> exchange of political views – Australians have turned from cutting
> down tall poppies to a punishing mood of small poppy resentment.

The media has helped to erode civic society, relying on:

> conflict and confrontation as the basis of popular entertainment,
> portraying winners and losers, majority and minority interests in
> every story. The mass media needs to be understood as another type
> of commerce, pitching its appeal to popular forms of entertainment.
> Within this framework, politics is presented as infotainment, while
> public issues are portrayed solely through a prism of conflict. This is
> why the electronic media spend so much time stereotyping unem-
> ployed people, welfare recipients and other subjects of downward

envy. Just as the Romans had the Colosseum, and Tudor England the village square stocks, we have *ACA* with Ray.

The first task for modern Labor, he says, is to return the commons to sustainability. This entails rebuilding "a common sense of public morality. [Labor] needs to strengthen the citizenry's commitment to membership and support of the public commons." Power and resources need to be decentralised, and in this way small groups sharing common interests will gain a direct understanding of the benefits of pooling resources, as well as the limits on these resources. The "raw size" of government has to be re-assessed. Boundaries and limits have to be visible and understandable by all.

> The success of the commons relies on a scale of organisation within which stakeholders are not only exposed to the behaviour of others but also have an appreciation of how their actions impact on the interests of others.

Following this logic, Latham goes on to argue for a pooling of federal and state government resources in health, education and welfare. "Place managers" and local authorities should decide how to use and distribute these resources. The "silos" of government departments have to be eliminated. The local area, rather than the centralised government agency, should be the organising unit. Implicit in and necessary to this is a rebuilding of civic society:

> The rise of downwards envy threatens the judgement about human values on which Labor is based: that people care about society enough to want to advance the interests of others, as well as themselves. It is the origin of wedge politics – reducing government and politics to a scramble for entitlements and scarce public entitlements, and politics to competition dividing and ruling … Unless the connection between individual action and collective consequences remains visible and direct, popular confidence in the management of the commons is bound to decline.

Latham's world-view is at heart an optimistic one. Just as villagers might come to an agreement on the use of common land, so modern citizens, once prized away from their television sets for long enough to meet the neighbours, might be able to agree on how to live together, and how the resources of their society are to be distributed. He also assumes, just as he did with the precinct committees in Liverpool, that ordinary citizens will want to be involved in matters of governance and politics, once they are made directly relevant to them.

If local communities are to take responsibility for the commons, there can be no freeloaders. The relationship between citizens and government has to be understood as one of mutual responsibility, not as one of patron and client. Passive welfare, Latham says, is not sustainable, either financially or socially. In *From the Suburbs*, Latham writes that the Labor agenda had to be "value-laden". The values, he suggests, come under four headings: responsibility, opportunity, community and democracy.

Latham is in favour of reassessing the scale of government agencies, but he is not in favour of small government in the sense of minimal government role. He is intensely pragmatic. He argues that government should not adopt ideologically fixed positions; rather its role should be to civilise the market and "enable" individuals and the community. How this might be done will vary over time and from place to place. Sometimes – but not often – it might mean government ownership of utilities and assets. At other times it might mean private companies or community groups delivering services usually associated with government. Ideology should be concerned with ends, not means, he says. Always, the scale of organisation should be kept small, local and visible.

Welfare

Latham argues that the welfare state was designed originally to provide short-term income support at times of job loss, old age and misfortune. Once, with full employment and earlier deaths, the welfare state was relatively cheap and certainly sustainable. Now the causes of poverty have become much more complex. It has become clear that the most effective kind of "welfare" is to find someone a job, but in some regions unemployment has become a way of life, communicated from generation to generation. This leads to a particular, self-perpetuating culture. Skills and self-esteem are eroded, and the disadvantaged lose the confidence and the ability to access resources in the way that other members of the community do. In *The Enabling State*, Latham attacked the then Employment Minister, Tony Abbott, for describing those who wouldn't move from $410 a week welfare benefits to a job worth $500 a week as bludgers and "job snobs":

> Abbott has a lot to learn about how the other half lives. All the evidence shows a close relationship between welfare dependency and social problems. Life on the dole is anything but quiet. It is associated with a host of anxieties and stresses, ranging from family problems, drugs and crime to a lack of education and hope in life.

People who don't get recognition from a job and a role in society obtain it in other ways, Latham says, including from subcultures in which drug use or car theft are the marks of adulthood:

> Welfare dependency is anything but a rational state of mind. Logic and responsiveness to financial incentives are replaced by an irrational and negative way of life.

The main drivers of dependency, Latham says, are social, not financial; they have their basis in the breakdown of self-esteem, recognition and trust: "At its core, long-term poverty is a problem in the relationship between people." Latham argues that the Labor Party needs to keep the idea of mutual responsibility in welfare. "Questions of social responsibility should not be regarded as the political property of the Right." He says Labor should distinguish itself by developing the idea that welfare is an active force, which helps recipients seize opportunities and develop.

Australia's welfare system should be completely redesigned on the basis of case and place management, he writes. All training and welfare payments from federal, state and local government should be pooled. In the most disadvantaged areas, other public resources – including those of health, housing, education and employment – may need to be bundled together and allocated by place managers. When allocating funds for housing and public infrastructure such as roads, government should have in mind the politics of place, and concentrate spending in areas of disadvantage.

"This structure", Latham acknowledges, "represents a fundamental overhaul of the federal system of government in Australia." Governments would be the funders. Place managers would be the purchasers, and would buy in mixes of services best suited to their area. Some services might be delivered by the public sector, others by the private sector or by welfare organisations; place managers could come from either sector. Latham writes at length about the changes that have been achieved by "social entrepreneurs" in disadvantaged areas, including areas of his own electorate. Social entrepreneurs are charismatic individuals, sometimes from government but more frequently from community groups, who set about "normalising" disadvantaged, crime-ridden neighbourhoods and creating connections and opportunities. True, he says, social entrepreneurs run on charisma, but this is not a reason for governments to back away from them. Rather governments need to find better ways of using charismatic individuals. They should be encouraged, not stifled.

Latham says the present welfare system is unsustainable and too complex. The Department of Social Security offers thirty-four different types of payment, each with its own eligibility criteria. Poverty traps are created which mean that individuals who find work are only marginally better off. The answer, Latham says, is a flexible, lifelong structure of income support based on both public funding and personal savings. The Department of Social Security would offer a menu of products – customised income-support packages – from which people could choose in much the same way they would sit down in front of a computer screen with a mortgage broker and select a home loan.

As well as this, Latham says, people need to plan for their own future financial security. Here he introduces an idea that recurs throughout his work — that of "forward savings" by individuals. He describes it as an extension of the principle of compulsory superannuation introduced by the Hawke-Keating government. These savings accounts — in the welfare context he calls them "income security accounts" or ISAs — would be managed in the same way as superannuation:

> On leaving education, people would apply for the establishment of an income security account, into which any social security entitle-ments would be paid. Subject to some prudential limitations, ISA holders would manage their entitlements. Those suffering chronic unemployment would have their entitlements case managed to build skill development and employment goals. People would be encouraged to make contributions to their accounts, and would not have to pay tax on these contributions. They could withdraw money, tax-free, to fund costs of economic restructuring, including education, retraining, child-care provisions, and income support. If after time the tax concession approach had proved insufficient to encourage strong levels of savings, it might be made mandatory … Funds could be brought forward from super, or deferred into super. At retirement, any ISA balance could be rolled into the superannu-ation pool.

Employment

The most urgent priority for overcoming disadvantage, Latham says, is employment. Although unemployment is at low levels nationwide, in certain areas it is up to 35 per cent. The globalised economy is not kind to disadvantaged areas. If disadvantage is to be overcome, he says, society cannot rely on reducing the wages of the lowest paid, or on labour market deregulation, or on assuming a "trickle-down" effect of economic growth:

> Low-skill neighbourhoods face a cycle of entrenched exclusion. Poor skills lead to long-term unemployment, low expectations and a running down of self-esteem. These problems, in turn, further diminish social and economic capability. When they pass from generation to generation, the neighbourhood itself and its history of educational under-achievement become an identifiable source of disadvantage. The problems of a suburb or region become much greater than the sum of its component parts might otherwise indicate.

In *Civilising Global Capital*, Latham proposes a new agenda for Labor's employment policy, with five related strategies. First, he says, government infrastructure development should be aimed at creating employment in regional and disadvantaged areas – "not short-term make-work schemes, but a long-term shift of resources". Government should also play a greater role in the provision of education, health, transport and childcare to such areas. Grants should be allocated on the basis of regional employment needs. The Commonwealth Grants Commission should be modified to make sure that state community-service programs are properly targetted.

Secondly, government should have a bigger role as an employer, paying people to do the kind of work once done by the charities and not-for-profit organisations now in decline. This should not be regarded as "work for the dole", but rather as a new "civic sector" of employment for the semi-skilled and non-skilled. Employers such as schools or community-based organisations would hire workers to provide meals on wheels, transport for frail elderly people and assistance at local schools, for example. The funds would come from both government and private sources. As a whole, the civic sector should be recognised and valued for providing real jobs that satisfy real social needs:

This requires in part a redefinition of the way society views employment. It requires government to resource the civic sector in a fashion no less legitimate than its conventional services. It requires the creation of a civic sector economy from which the attainment of full employment is a social priority.

Thirdly, Latham advocates workplace solidarity, and a reinvigoration both of centralised wage fixing and the role of unions. Research, he claims, shows that unionised workforces earn more. For the bottom tier of workplaces, individual employment contracts and the erosion of collective bargaining strength have led to more insecurity and inequality.

He proposes a two-tier wages system. Internationally competitive workers should have their wages tied to productivity gains. The second group — those workers without the skills to feel secure in the globalised economy — should have minimum wages guaranteed, with the "floor" reflecting the costs of "active citizenship" rather than arbitrary and inadequate poverty lines. Latham rejects the argument that wage movements beyond the gains of productivity have the effect of pricing workers out of jobs. Labour, he says, is not just another commodity like fish and chips. American research, he says, has shown that the conventional models are wrong: an increase in minimum wages does not lead to more unemployment. Sometimes it even has the reverse effect. He proposes a formal, indexed link between the living wage and general movements in earnings.

Latham's fourth strategy for achieving full employment is support for co-operative financial institutions that allow retrenched workers to pool their savings and redundancy payouts to invest in new industries and markets. "Labour hiring capital, rather than the other way round," he says.

Finally, Latham turns to corporate responsibility. He rejects the idea that corporations should be amoral, interested only in maximising profits. Government policy needs to ensure that capital serves the needs of society. The ideal of mutual obligation should apply to corporate citizens as much as to individuals. The federal government should force banks to meet minimum standards for face-to-face banking services. Recipients of "corporate welfare" should be obliged to guarantee that money will be spent to create employment. Subsidies to corporations should be clawed back if they fail to deliver on these guarantees.

Education

Education is the area in which Latham's ideas are most developed. He describes the government's role as a funder of education as the most important form of interaction between state and citizenry, and the main instrument for equipping both individuals and the country to deal with change. Education "reignites the role of government as a force for social equity". It is the "fulcrum on which income security rests". He even suggests that education should be the focus for a new sense of patriotism: in a world where the boundaries that used to constrain finance have disappeared, education and research are "a core source of national sovereignty". Countries that do not invest sufficiently in education are at the mercy of international markets, while countries that invest in "human capital" retain some control over their destinies. Money will always follow the skilled workers, which is one of the reasons, he says, why poverty is localised and self-perpetuating.

For all of these reasons, education cannot be left to market forces. The market will not deliver equity and effective choice:

> If education is purchased and sold like any other market commodity, it is reduced solely to the status of a private good, denying society its opportunity to maximise the public-good features of lifelong learning.

On the other hand, Latham says the Whitlam approach – full government funding of tertiary education – is no longer sustainable. When Whitlam abolished tertiary fees, few Australians expected to go to university. Financing higher education was comparatively cheap. Now tertiary education or training is a near-universal requirement.

The title of Latham's book *What Did You Learn Today?* was taken from the British educationalist Michael Barber, who suggested that instead of asking the icebreaker question, "What do you do for a living?" we would in the future ask, "What did you learn today?" Latham claims to have tried it. "It not only leads to more interesting conversations, it gives a useful insight into the habits of a learning society."

Education, Latham says, should not be confined to institutions. "Society needs to become absorbed by education, both in the attainment of formal qualifications and in the popular practice of community-based learning." Learning should take place in pubs, clubs, schools after hours, in the workplace, the home and wherever people gather for a public purpose. Digital television should be harnessed to the cause, and interactive education packages offered at libraries, post offices and schools. Learning, Latham said, should be customised. It would be silly to plan for equal outcomes. Rather the public sector should help each individual to fulfil his or her potential.

Latham argues that education has to begin from birth, with parents reading to children. Pre-school should be the norm, if not compulsory for four-year-olds, and efforts should be made to identify and help children with learning difficulties as soon as possible, before they begin formal schooling.

Turning to schools, he argues that devoting more resources to "a one-size-fits-all system" will not address the inequalities that divide the children of educated parents from those who come from disadvantaged neighbourhoods. Disadvantaged areas require customised solutions. The best teachers should be sent to such areas, and these students might have to be in the classroom for longer and do more home study than those from other areas. Parents might need to be trained to be effective educators, perhaps with courses at the school itself. The responsibility to be effective home educators should be written into case-management contracts for chronic social security recipients.

The responsibility for setting curriculum should be taken away from state governments, and all schools should be required to meet minimum national standards as a condition of government funding. Once minimum standards are reached, diversity should be encouraged. Disadvantaged schools should become neighbourhood learning and support centres, drawing resources from across the community. They might host breakfast clubs and homework centres. They would be a centre for "pastoral care" of children and families. Throughout Australia, parents should be helped to set up community schools, and encouraged to contribute to these financially and in kind – by looking after the grounds and helping in the classroom. Funding for schools should be based on need, Latham says, regardless of whether the school is public or private. However, the capacity of parents to pay school fees should be factored into funding decisions. Not all schools should get public funding. If the fee-paying capacity of the parents is high enough for the school to reach national standards, then government funding should go to schools in greater need. The total pool of funding would therefore increase.

Post-secondary education or training should be near-universal. "In the new economy, there are few, if any jobs for unskilled teenagers." No Australian school leaver should be deterred from continuing his or her education for financial reasons, he says. This will mean softening the financial impact of Higher Education Contribution Scheme fees (HECS) and providing greater income support for students. Loan schemes are not enough, as those from disadvantaged areas are less likely to seek education if it means taking on loans they do not feel confident of repaying.

Here Latham once again suggests the idea of forward savings, in the form of "Lifelong Learning Accounts". These would be started from birth with government money, and could be built up through individual contributions and salary-sacrifice schemes. These accounts could be drawn upon to pay HECS fees, for income support while studying, to buy computers and internet connections for school students, or to pay for retraining later in life.

Latham argues for the abolition of the "two-tier" tertiary education system introduced by the Howard government, in which full-fee-paying students can obtain a university place with a lower tertiary score. "It sends an appalling message to a generation of young Australians. If their parents are wealthy, some students might think they do not have to study or work as hard at school."

Higher education, Latham wrote in 2001, needs to be rethought from first principles. At present it is governed by:

> a bland, hybrid culture of management which, due to the down-grading of public funds, has been forced to combine commercial pressure with the traditional hierarchies of university life. This hybrid has produced the worst of all worlds. The original ideal of the university as a community of scholars has been lost. The contemporary demand for creative and entrepreneurial university leadership also remains unfulfilled.

Instead he proposes a mixed system of regulation and funding. Federal government would develop a national policy framework, and universities would lodge expressions of intent, and nominate how they would prefer to be funded. A new body, the Australian Universities Commission, would negotiate individual agreements and monitor performance. Latham wrote in *What Did You Learn Today?* that six different kinds of universities might emerge. There would be free public universities focussed on regional development and equity programs, and with close links with TAFE and industry. These would get a big increase in public funding, and might well become the most financially secure institutions. Secondly, specialist universities might focus on particular courses and areas, such as liberal arts, advanced technology, and teaching and research excellence. These would be funded by a mixture of government money and HECS contributions. Other universities would scarcely change from the present model, offering comprehensive courses and funded from a mixture of private and public money, including HECS. International universities would rely on fees from overseas students and private revenue, and might offer means-tested scholarships. Research universities would work in combination with advanced industry, similar to Stanford University's role in California's Silicon Valley. Finally, there will be a group of flexible universities defined by their relationships with other organisations, such as the Australian Catholic University, or universities closely tied to big corporations.

Health

Perhaps the most politically explosive ideas in Latham's books concern health-care, and in particular health insurance. He proposes a system that would mean the radical restructure, probably even the abolition, of Medicare, which for years has been one of Labor's strongest political causes. However he remains in favour of universal, government-funded quality health-care.

Latham says that since Whitlam established Medibank, health-care has changed fundamentally. New technology means higher costs and higher expectations, but it has also created opportunities to manage health spending more effectively. It is now possible to assess accurately the likely health costs for specific groups in the population, and the costs of treating various kinds of diseases and injuries. Public policy has not kept pace, he says. There has been incremental reform when what is needed is a fresh approach, and an end to the struggle between free markets and public providers. "Ownership issues have obscured the importance of outcomes." Free markets cannot work in health-care, Latham asserts, because they depart too much from the basic goals of access and equity. Public monopolies, on the other hand, suffer from lack of efficiency and lack of responsiveness to consumer preferences.

The answer, he argues, is a "third way" based on regional and case management. Australia, Latham says, has one of the most complex health systems in the world. Federal government has sixty separate health programs, which the state systems criss-cross and overlap. There is endless cost- and blame-shifting between the levels of government. Most Australians need health-care only intermittently, he says, but for 10 per cent or so of the population, health-care is a daily fact of life. These people need many services from many programs and levels of government. Under the present system, it is impossible to guarantee equity between regions and states, or to co-ordinate care of chronically ill individuals.

Latham proposes that state, federal and local government health resources be gathered into a single pool and distributed to regional authorities. The Commonwealth would shed direct service responsibilities but remain responsible for equity between regions. States, through regional authorities, would be responsible for all service delivery. Case-mix funding, in which hospitals are paid for the kind of work they have done rather than on the basis of their fixed costs, should be introduced nationwide. Meanwhile, purchaser and provider functions would be split. Regional health authorities would buy in services, provided by government agencies or private industry.

Latham argues that health insurance should be completely recast. Technology and data processing now make it possible to estimate with great accuracy the likely health-care needs of different groups of citizen. Governments could fulfil its commitment to universal health-care by making a risk-rated payment for each citizen. These payments, with the option for top-ups or privately funded supplements, could be used to purchase the health plan best suited to the needs of the consumer. Health-services brokers would be available to advise and put together packages in the same way that travel agents advise on the best holiday package. Some consumers might choose to pool their funds and establish co-operatives, which could then employ their own general practitioners or offer preventative health programs. This would be, Latham acknowledges, a revival of the "Friendly Societies" that existed before Medibank.

In an appendix to *Civilising Global Capital*, Latham proposes a five-stage introduction of his new health system. Stage One would be a pooling of the health resources of federal and state governments, together with the development of new patient information systems. Stage Two would see the implementation of regional health management, with all services fully integrated under national equity and access standards. Stage Three would introduce payment to service providers on an output basis – case-mix funding. Stage Four would see the phased introduction of the purchaser/provider split, making public and private providers compete for contracts from regional health authorities. Finally, most health consumers would become members of health insurance co-operatives, while "chronic users" of the health system would be under the management of "care agents" who would custom-design a mix of services.

Taxation

Perhaps Latham's most radical proposal in *Civilising Global Capital* is a fresh approach to taxation. Latham proposes a system based on the work of British economist Nicholas Kaldor, under which taxes are levied not on income, but on consumption.

Taxpayers would still fill out annual tax returns, but they would be taxed not on their income, but on their consumption. That is, they would be taxed on the money they had earned *minus* any savings or investments. Tax would be levied at progressive rates, set to ensure that the biggest consumers paid the highest proportion of tax. The Kaldor tax is therefore very different from the GST.

The Kaldor system, Latham argued, would focus government revenue-raising on the activities conducted in Australia. It would end tax avoidance by corporations shifting income off-shore. At the same time high marginal rates would not act as a disincentive to earning, but would discourage lavish consumption and encourage saving and investment.

In *Civilising Global Capital*, Latham acknowledges that the Kaldor system has not been implemented anywhere in the world, but claims it is well suited to Australia, partly because taxpayers here are accustomed to making annual taxation returns (a stumbling block elsewhere). The reforms involved in introducing the Kaldor system would be radical, he acknowledges, but:

Social democracy is rapidly losing the comfort of the do-nothing option. If it does not restore the bases and fairness of the revenue system, then inevitably the political right will be able to further develop and implement its agenda for regressive and indirect forms of tax.

*

Latham's thinking seems to me to be clearly reflected in the few policies Labor has released so far. In April this year, the Shadow Health Minister, Julia Gillard, announced that Labor would in the first month of a new government establish a National Health Reform Commission, headed by "an expert in change management". Within three months, a summit would be held to bring together practitioners and governments at all levels. She went on to outline the ideas that might be considered by the summit; included among them were the pooling of state and federal money and the use of "smartcard" technology to track the costs of health-care. Since then, both Gillard and (shortly afterwards) the Health Minister, Tony Abbott, have announced plans for a new-generation Medicare smartcard that contains basic health information. It is tempting to see these moves as Stage One of the five-part program for change that Latham outlined in *Civilising Global Capital*. Meanwhile Labor has promised to retain but improve the government subsidy for private health insurance, and to safeguard Medicare. So far there are no details. Could it be that this will be done by making the "risk-rated payments" that Latham foreshadowed as part of his proposed re-casting of private health insurance?

In the area of education, Labor has announced that it will introduce a needs-based funding model for schools with uniform national standards. Wealthy schools will get less, but most independent schools will be better off, Latham has said. In tertiary education, Latham has promised the abolition of positions for Australian full-fee-paying students. He has said he plans to reverse the Howard government's recent moves to allow institutions to increase HECS, and that his government will increase government funding to universities and TAFEs.

The university funding model Latham outlined in *What Did You Learn Today?* is in fact similar in thrust, if not in detail, to the scheme negotiated and introduced by the Howard government's Education Minister, Brendan Nelson. Latham's approach differs chiefly in that he wants to reduce rather than to increase fees, and also wants some "free" universities entirely funded by government.

Other policies announced by Labor also reflect the ideas in Latham's books. There is the "mentorships" program for young people, and a banking policy with an emphasis on corporate responsibility. A housing policy, released in the middle of all the fuss about Latham's buck's night and largely overlooked by the media, promises a big boost in Commonwealth funding for public housing, a reinvigorated agreement with the states, and partnerships between government and locally based community groups, aimed both at building homes and at overcoming unemployment in disadvantaged areas. Meanwhile Labor's industrial relations policy has been one of the main areas of real controversy in the campaign so far. Labor's platform calls for the restoration of the right to collective bargaining, and the abolition of Australian Workplace Agreements, which allow conditions to be set at below-award levels. Labor has also promised to give the Industrial Relations Commission more power to arbitrate disputes. Not all these policies are Latham's work. They were part of the party's platform before he became leader. Together, they represent a halt, if not a rolling back, of the deregulation of the labour market pursued by both the Hawke-Keating and the Howard governments. Perhaps it is a precursor to a version of the two-tier system Latham outlined in *Civilising Global Capital* – with more regulation and security for the less well skilled, and productivity-based wage increases for the internationally competitive.

The last section of Latham's big book concerns "social capital", the resources of trust, respect and co-operation that societies draw upon in order to pursue individual and collective interests. Latham says there are two forms of social capital – "vertical", which is based in respect for and trust in hierarchies, and "horizontal", which relies on trust and co-operation between equals, without compulsion or sacrifice of freedom.

Australia, he says, has never been good at the latter, "horizontal" form of solidarity. We still suffer from having been founded as a penal colony, in which the government held all the power. Australia was a "born modern" state, without the centuries of community co-operation developed in Europe long before the advent of big government. In support of this, Latham refers to a 1996 survey by Liverpool City Council into the social values and lifestyle interests of middle Australia. The survey, he writes, told a story of over-geared mortgages, hand-to-mouth living and disengagement from formally organised institutions "One of the councillors described the results as reflecting a 'do not disturb' generation." Searching Australian history for an "identifiable form of horizontal social capital", Latham could find only one – the ideal of Australian mateship.

Australian Labor, he says, has neglected social capital, and with it the oldest form of socialism, the trust and mutuality shared by people who live together. Modern Labor has dealt instead with big institutions, big government and abstracts:

> It is now too readily forgotten that the socialist cause commenced as a social creed in search of mutuality and self-sufficiency. It was not necessarily assumed, however, that the achievement of these goals required a large and centralised scale of state provision. This only arose as a consequence of state socialist ideology ... Early Left thinking, such as the ideals of guild socialism, was heavily influenced by the possibilities of a smaller scale of public mutuality. This ideology was expressed through attempts to create a new type of production system: the development of self-governing guilds in the workplace, similar to what we would now think of as industrial democracy.

Latham ends his big book by talking about the need for politicians – particularly Labor Party politicians – to engage the population in a "civic conversation". It is an extension of the idea he had first aired at Liverpool

Council with the precinct committees, and which he has carried forward into his present career with his use of the community-forum method of campaigning.

Had Mark Latham granted me an interview, an obvious question would have been whether he still subscribed to the ideas in *Civilising Global Capital* and his other books, and if not, why not. Does he still believe, for example, that a Kaldor consumption tax is feasible and desirable in Australia? Does he still want to revive health insurance "Friendly Societies"?

Civilising Global Capital – and all of Latham's books – are written by a man with great faith in human nature. He takes as a given that people want, not only to better themselves, but also to be active members of a community. He takes for granted a desire for decency and the welfare of others.

I would have liked to ask him what he thinks of the election campaign so far. Given the buck's night video fiasco and his visit to *Big Brother*, I would be very interested to know how Mark Latham thinks the civic conversation is going.

Before Paul Keating lost government in 1996, he said that politics does matter, and so do leaders. "Change the government and you change the country," he asserted, and few would disagree.

The conventional analysis of Australian history sees the nation as partly characterised and partly goaded into the future by its leaders. From Menzies through Whitlam, Fraser, Hawke, Keating and Howard, each leader has spun us a yarn about who we are, both as Australians and as human beings. They have also told us something about what we might aspire to be. Each is remembered by phrases and speeches – sometimes just snippets of language – that, with the passage of time, seemed to sum up both the leaders and the people who elected them. There was Menzies' "forgotten people", and his allegiance to Britain. There was Whitlam's plain, cut-down prose, his appeal to a matter-of-fact, egalitarian sense of national identity – "men and women of Australia". There was Fraser's air of small "l" liberal grace-under-pressure – "life wasn't meant to be easy." There was Hawke's rhetoric of consensus, and Keating's true believers. Keating thought, according to his biographer Don Watson, that Australia might well become a "nice little country", by which he meant democratic, prosperous, liberal, fair and, most difficult of all, finally reconciled with its brutal history. Howard, surely, will be remembered for the phrase "relaxed and comfortable". Whereas Keating asserted that Australia still had a big job of reconciliation and self-examination to do before we could become "nice", John Howard rejected the "black armband" historians. In Howard's view, we were already "nice", and had been since at least the 1950s.

"One of the more insidious developments in Australian political life over the past decade or so has been the attempt to rewrite Australian history in the service of a partisan political cause," Howard said shortly after his triumph in 1996.

The cliché says that victors write history. I think John Howard has taken this to heart, but feared that it might be true in a way not normally understood. He has worried, not so much that victors write history, but that the writers of history *become* the victors, no matter what their political success. I think he has understood all too well the power of books and ideas, and has feared that the left intellectual elite will win in the end, not by gaining government but by determining the vocabulary and the context in which his record will be assessed. So it is that Howard has presided over the culture wars. Those on "his" side assert that no guilt, self-examination or agonising are needed. "As a nation we are over all that sort of identity stuff," he has said. And on another occasion:

> We no longer navel-gaze about what an Australian is. We no longer are mesmerised by the self-appointed cultural dieticians who tell us that in some way they know better what an Australian ought to be than all of us who know what an Australian has always been and always will be.

The result of the culture wars is, surely, that the left intellectual elite will never again be able to take for granted their domination of the yarn-spinning, rhetorical side of public life. They will never again be able to take for granted the kind of victory that comes from writing history.

John Howard's political success and Mark Latham's ascension to power force a re-examination of Keating's assertion that changing governments changes the country. The last eight years have taught us that, in fact, the country did not change as much under Keating as some of us thought it had. The Hawke-Keating years did not make us reconciled to our history, nor did they advance the bulk of Australians much in that direction. Keating failed to convince most Australians of a need for reconciliation, let alone instil a passion for its achievement. His famous Redfern speech – moving, urgent, remorseful, a word-song – did nothing but alienate most Australians. Four years after the Redfern speech came the voice of the reaction, when Pauline Hanson made her maiden speech to Federal Parliament. Her language too was cut-down, shunning abstracts, a thin but steel-strong assertion of rights:

> I am fed up with being told, "This is our land." Well, where the hell
> do I go? I was born here, and so were my parents and children …
> I draw the line when told I must pay and continue paying for some-
> thing that happened over two hundred years ago. Like most
> Australians, I worked for my land; no one gave it to me.

Howard's first response was to express pleasure that, once again, it was possible for this kind of thing to be said. He understood that this too was a narrative. This too was a powerful speech. For many Australians, this was the thing.

Globalisation, an irresistible force, has changed Australia but has not changed the most Australians' attitudes to the world. Most Australians still respond to assertions of sovereignty and sameness, such as Howard's "We decide who comes here, and the circumstances under which they come." Perhaps the call is all the stronger because we sense, in our hearts, that if capital is footloose, then there is no logic to resist the idea that labour – people – might also travel the world in search of better opportunities. And what would Australia be then?

It seems to me that both Keating and Howard have been peddling a kind of fiction. We are not the people Keating wanted us to be. Not yet, in any case, and perhaps we never will be. The words that stirred the hearts of the insiders alienated the outsiders. Keating carries a share of responsibility for the success of John Howard. On the other hand, Howard also peddles fiction. It is self-evident that we are not, and cannot be, "relaxed and comfortable". We may be prosperous as a nation, but we have also never been more divided. Poverty is concentrated geographi-cally, so most of us never have to confront it. Nevertheless, it is there. We are developing an underclass. At the same time, ordinary workers have never felt more insecure. Only those who are very well equipped to deal with change can feel confident that life will be comfortable in the future. In post-war Australia, the path has never been steeper, nor more slippery. And all this insecurity is without even beginning to take into account new threats, such as terrorism and war and a powerful ally that believes in the justice of the pre-emptive strike.

One of the things that people like me – readers, writers, undoubtedly members of the chattering classes – tend to find most disturbing about Australia's great suburban spaces is the apparent lack of a story. As Latham observes, the big, flat western suburbs of Sydney, and their counterparts in all the state capitals, are pragmatic, small-picture places. There are gestures, of course, towards big stories – "family" and "community" tend to be words thrown to the wind. "Home" is one of the most powerful symbols of all. Also, the statistics tell us, those who live on the fringes are more likely than the rest of us to be church-goers. But conversations on abstracts and the transcendental tend to tail off out here, and return to the pragmatic. Most of Australia's thinkers and writers, to their shame, have failed to find inspiration in the Australian suburbs. Mark Latham is an exception. In his first book – the one advocating reform of the Labor Party on a local basis – Latham concludes his acknowledgements by saying, "As ever, Liverpool was an enduring inspiration." Mark Latham found his big and small pictures out there. The title of his most recent book encapsulates this: *From the Suburbs – Building a Nation from Our Neighbourhoods*.

Mark Latham speaks to the people who were alienated by Keating – the ones who probably didn't want to change at all, and yet have been forced by economic pressure to do so. He represents pragmatism, yet also an appeal to values. He tells people they are not selfish to focus on their own neighbourhoods, and on their relationships to their neighbours, rather than on "big pictures" and people very different from themselves. He believes in facing things squarely. His weaknesses are self-evident. He is a good hater. He has, in the past, lacked wisdom in his dealings with people. The other side of that coin is that he has phenomenal political courage. He is almost "crazy-brave" – in a political sense a gambler, like his father.

He lacks a capacity for abstract thought. On the other hand, he is surely one of the most penetrating analytical thinkers of recent Australian history, and one of very few thinkers to achieve political leadership. It is not his credentials as a thinker that are in doubt, but his capacity to build alliances, to persuade, to take people with him, to truly lead and to build things that endure.

There is an irony to Latham's political success so far – almost a paradox. He has achieved leadership and popularity largely because the nation has not changed as much as we thought it had, but at the same time he is himself a merchant of radical change. Whether he can transform the country is not only a matter of his abilities. To bring about change is always a very difficult thing, and there is little reason to think that Australians are convinced of the need for the back-to-first-principles thinking that Latham represents. For decades, voters have been told that the main job of politicians is to manage the economy – a topic in which few voters feel qualified. I doubt if Latham will be able to convince them that it is now acceptable to vote on the basis of social issues, and the concrete things that directly affect their lives, however much they might want to. I may be wrong about this. If Latham wins this election, it will signal an end to the domination of economists, and a revival of a social agenda

I think what I like about Mark Latham most of all is that he is an optimist. He sees the Labor Party as the party of optimism. It has been said that John Howard has succeeded because he sees us exactly as we are. I think the same is true of Mark Latham. The difference between the two men is Latham's optimism. He believes in human beings, and in human nature. He believes in tolerance not as an abstract ideal, but as a real product of civic connectedness. He believes that we can live together well, and he believes that we can succeed in a fast-changing world and be the better for it. He wants us to be, not relaxed and comfortable, but active and engaged.

Mark Latham's arrival on the political scene has brought to an end the fictions that have dominated politics for the last ten years. Whatever lies ahead – and whether or not Mark Latham wins government – we have at last arrived in our present.

SOURCES

This essay was informed by numerous interviews. Many of the subjects, particularly those from within Labor Party circles, did not wish to be named. "On-the-record" interview subjects included Gabrielle Gwyther, Nick Whitlam, Gough Whitlam, Julia Gillard, Dr Robert Jones, Evan Thornley, Casey Conway, John Walker, John Button, Joan Kirner, Senator Bob Brown and Michael Byrne. I thank them all, perhaps especially those who will not be pleased with the final result. I would also like to thank the staff of Liverpool City Council, and reporters employed by the News Limited suburban chains, Messenger Newspapers, Leader Newspapers and Cumberland Newspapers, for insights into the impact of Mark Latham's community forums.

3   Latham described himself as a "club buster" in interviews with the *Liverpool Champion*, 18 July 1987, and the *Liverpool Leader*, 19 January 1994.

5   Latham's description of Labor as a party of outsiders is in Chapter One of his book *From the Suburbs: Building a Nation from Our Neighbourhoods*, Pluto Press, Annandale, NSW, 2003. This chapter is based on the Menzies Lecture 2002, "Wedge Politics and the Culture War in Australia", delivered by Latham on 17 September 2002 and published by the Menzies Centre for Australian Studies, King's College, London, 2003.

6   Latham's ideas about Part One and Part Two and multiple identity citizenship are outlined in the book he co-edited with Peter Botsman, *The Enabling State: People before Bureaucracies*, Pluto Press, Annandale, NSW, 2001.

6   Shirley Hazzard was interviewed by Jane Cornwell in the *Australian*, 18 June 2004, under the title "Literal Search for the Truth".

10   Mark Latham's comments about his father and about being a "mummy's boy" were made in a report for *60 Minutes* by Charles Wooley, 14 March 2004. Similar remarks were reported by Bernard Lagan in an article, "The Fight Stuff", *Bulletin*, 26 November 2003; and by Craig McGregor in his book *Australian Son − Inside Mark Latham*, Pluto Press, North Melbourne, Vic., 2004. Latham's sister Jody's remarks, and other insights into Don Latham, were contained in an article by Christine Jackman published in the *Weekend Australian Magazine*, 20 March 2004. For Lorraine Latham's comments about Gough Whitlam being a second father to Mark, see Tony Stephens, "Elder Statesmen Anoint Their Napoleon", *Sydney Morning Herald*, 3 December 2003.

10   Gough Whitlam's book *The Whitlam Government 1972–1975* was published by Penguin, Ringwood, Vic., 1985.

13   Latham's book *Civilising Global Capital – New Thinking for Australian Labor* was published by Allen & Unwin, St Leonards, NSW, 1998.

13   Latham's "arselicker" comment about Howard was published in an interview with Maxine McKew in the *Bulletin*, 26 June 2002. Abbott responded on ABC Radio's *The World Today*, 26 June 2002.

14   Gorton's remark about Whitlam was published in the *Sydney Morning Herald*, and is quoted in *The Whitlam Government 1972–1975*.

14   Latham's book *Reviving Labor's Agenda: A Program for Local Reform* was published by Pluto Press and the Australian Fabian Society, Leichhardt, NSW, 1990.

16   The interview with Latham about Whitlam was published in the *Liverpool Champion*, 24 July 1985.

17   Whitlam's role in organising Latham's trip to PNG was reported by Shane McLeod on ABC Radio's *AM*, 26 February 2004.

17   Latham's ideas about "The Third Way" are most clearly stated in *The Enabling State*, which also contains his "guiding ideology" quote.

18   Noel Pearson described Latham's ideas as his main inspiration in *The Enabling State*.

20   Gough Whitlam's visit to Emerald was reported in the *Central Queensland News* of 5 December 1974.

25   Latham's challenge to Howard on the community forums was reported in *Hansard* for 23 June 2004.

27   Latham's analysis of the culture wars is contained in the Menzies Lecture 2002, "Wedge Politics and the Culture War in Australia" and in Chapter One of *From the Suburbs*.

28   The 2001 Australian Electoral Study is quoted in Burchell's book *Western Horizon: Sydney's Heartland and the Future of Australian Politics*, Scribe, Carlton North, Vic., 2003. I am also indebted to Burchell for elements of my analysis of the "insiders" and "outsiders" issue and the nature of our outer suburbs.

32   Marcia Langton's attack on the Left was published in *Overland*, No. 166, Autumn 2002.

33   Latham's remarks about the chattering classes are found in "Social Inclusiveness in an Open Economy", *Labor Essays 1997: Renewing and Revitalising Labor*, ed. Gary Jungwirth, Pluto Press Australia in association with the Australian Fabian Society, Sydney, 1997.

34   Latham's use in parliament of the phrase "the forgotten people", and Howard's response, occurred on 12 May 2004. Latham's comments on Menzies' "Forgotten People" speech are found in *From the Suburbs*.

34   Whitlam's comments on the arts as an end in themselves are taken from *The Whitlam Government 1972–1975*.

35   Mal Logan's remarks come from his essay "Reflections", published in the *Australian*'s forty years anniversary series, Part 3: Knowledge, 21 July 2004.

36   The local papers I read in Caboolture were the *Sunshine Coast Daily*, 19 May 2004; the *Caboolture Shire Herald*, 18 May 2004; the *Caboolture News*, 19 May 2004; and the *Northern Times*, 14 May 2004.

43   Malcolm Schmidtke and Gay Alcorn's profile of Mark Latham was published in the *Age*, 12 March 2004.

43   The *Australian*'s report on the taxi driver was "No grudge, but no vote, from cabbie", 3 December 2003.

44–48   The *Sunday* program's profile of Mark Latham was screened on Sunday, 4 July 2004. Latham's interview with John Laws took place on 2 July. The *Australian* editorial was published on 3 July. Crikey.com.au went public in their mail-out to subscribers on 2 July. Louise Dodson's article was published in the *Sydney Morning Herald* on 3 July. Lincoln Wright's article ran in News Limited newspapers on 4 July. Glen Milne's article ran in News Limited newspapers on 3 July. Damien Murphy and Deborah Snow's article was published in the *Sydney Morning Herald*, 12 July 2004. Matt Price's comment on this article was published in the *Australian*, 17 July 2004.

50   Gabrielle Gwyther's work on Sydney's aspirational suburbs includes "Socio-spatial Differentiation and the Master Planned Community in a Global City", Research Paper 8, Urban Frontiers Program, University of Western Sydney, April 2002. Published at http://www.uq.edu.au/csrc/delfin/relatedpapers/Gwyther2002.pdf.

51   Latham's admission about his treatment of his enemies at Liverpool is taken from the transcript of his press conference held on 5 July 2004.

55   Information about the history of Liverpool and of Glen Alpine is taken from the websites of the Liverpool City Council and the Campbelltown City Council respectively: www.liverpool.nsw.gov.au and www.campbelltown.nsw.gov.au.

58   Casey Conway's 1988 criticism of Latham was reported in the *Liverpool Fairfield Champion*, 8 June 1988.

61–69   The account of Latham's period as a councillor and mayor is based largely on articles published in the *Liverpool Leader* over the relevant period, together with interviews with Michael Byrne, Casey Conway and other Liverpool identities.

69   Dr Robert Jones' research has been published as follows: Jones, Robert and Gross, Michael, "A Tale of Two Councils: Strategic Change in Australian Local Government", *Strategic Change*, Vol.5, pp.123–139, 1996.

Jones, Robert and Gross, Michael, "Best Practice in Cultural Change in NSW Local Government", Research Report submitted to the READ Foundation Institute of Municipal Management, September 1997.

Jones, Robert, "Implementing Decentralised Reform in Local Government – Leadership Lessons from the Australian Experience", *International Journal of Public Sector Management*, Vol.12, No.1, 1999, pp.63–76.

Other material has been drawn from my interview with Dr Jones, and his unpublished transcripts and notes of interviews with John Walker and other Liverpool City Council staff.

70–73   My discussion of the Liverpool City Council finances and management is drawn from:

Liverpool City Council Annual Reports 1991–1997/8.

Comparative Information on New South Wales Local Government Councils 1994/95; 1995/96, published by the NSW Department of Local Government.

General Manager's Report to Liverpool City Council Ordinary Meeting, 13 September 1993.

Letter from Colin Harrington to Piers Akerman, 18 June 2004, detailing information given to Harrington by Liverpool City Council financial staff.

My own interviews with Liverpool City Council officers.

73   The Report and transcripts of evidence of the Oasis Inquiry into Liverpool City Council are published at http://www.dlg.nsw.gov.au/liverpool.

76   Mark Latham's claims about his management of Liverpool City Council were made in parliament on 1 June 2004.

80   Greg Sheridan's description of Latham's ideas was published in the *Australian*, 11 December 2003.

81   David Burchell commented on Latham's record as a thinker in "Politics: The Right Idea", *Australian Policy OnLine*, 10 February 2004, http://www.apo.org.au. It was this article that alerted me to Sheridan's views.

81–102 The summary of Latham's ideas is drawn mainly from *Civilising Global Capital*, with additional material from *What Did You Learn Today?: creating an education revolution*, Allen & Unwin, Crows Nest, NSW, 2001, *The Enabling State* and *From the Suburbs*.

103   Don Watson wrote about the "nice little country" in *Recollections of a Bleeding Heart: A Portrait of Paul Keating PM*, Knopf, Milsons Point, NSW, 2002. Watson also quotes Keating's "change the government and you change the country" remark.

104   The quotes from John Howard are taken from James Curran's book *The Power of Speech — Australian Prime Ministers Defining the National Image*, Melbourne University Press, Carlton, Vic., 2004.

ACKNOWLEDGING DIFFERENCE

| *Public Intellectuals and Aboriginal Australia*

Inga Clendinnen

The inaugural *Quarterly Essay* Lecture was delivered on 1 May 2004 as part of the Readings @ Mietta's literary festival.

I used to think you got to be a "public intellectual" through discreet self-advertisement oiled by secret vanity. I now discover it is thrust upon you by persons unknown, and that there is no job-description: you have to learn on the job. Most of you in this hall are in the business of creating, disseminating or consuming opinions on social matters. It is the un-rehearsed responsibilities of the opinion providers I want to talk about this morning.

My recognition of the awkwardness of our condition came out of a question asked at the Sydney Writers' Festival last year. Academic conferences tend to be dull affairs because everyone present is a professional, and everyone plays by the rules. Writers' festivals aren't like that. What they are most like is improvised theatre, with everyone, on stage and off, an amateur. The formal topic for this particular session was Rosemary Neill's book *White Out: How Politics Is Killing Black Australia*, but the real plot-line was how the three Aboriginal men on the panel would respond to their two (white, female) fellow-panellists and their (largely white) audience: whether some sufficiently reassuring representation of reconciliation would be acted out on the stage.

Rosemary, who spoke first, stuck resolutely to an account of her intentions in writing the book. Then the senior man spoke. He was about my age – a bit younger – and he had already lived about five biographies to my one. He had just been awarded a Ph.D. in an academic career he began when he was over fifty. I have been at school since I was six.

In effect, he told us to leave him and his people alone: that we were ignorant, and dangerous in our ignorance. The second man said much the same thing rather more gently, adding that, by contrast with his people, we were horribly culturally impoverished. The third was a poet and, in the gracious way of poets, entrusted us with one of his poems, although it was pretty clear that he expected his few Aboriginal listeners to understand it better than we did. I spoke last; tried to extract some encouraging message out of all this; failed. These people had had enough not only of white malice, and white neglect. They had had enough of white interference, and even of white goodwill.

As we shuffled out into the rain a woman spoke to me. She said, with a kind of despairing self-disgust I recognised: "I'm white, I'm middle-class, I live here in Sydney, and I cannot bear what is happening. What can I do?" She was almost weeping. I muttered something about "educating ourselves to be prepared for political action, if the time for action ever comes". Even to me it sounded hollow. She has been on my conscience ever since. Today I want to try to give her a better answer. What had we been up to, you and I, and what could we do differently?

I am sure that this woman, like so many others, had been roused by the *Bringing them home* report. Whatever the defects of that report – under-researched because under-funded, selective, "political" – there can be no doubt of the impact of its stories. Humans have a unique talent for stories: for telling them, and for learning from them. They are our most economical technique for expanding experience. Hearing them, we have the sense that we can stand, that we are indeed standing, in another person's shoes. When the stories are true, that experience is a powerful incitement to action. The *Bringing them home* stories were true, and almost unbearably poignant. So what did *we* do with the moral and political energies they roused?

What we mainly did was to try to classify muddled intentions and actions under large concepts to render them apt for moral judgement. That is, by and large, what public intellectuals are expected to do. One obvious example: we unleashed a controversy about the applicability of the term "genocide" to what had been done here, and then about what adjectival qualifier – "cultural"? "occasional", "sporadic"? – was appropriate. We also engaged in politics, trying to force a narrow and stubborn man to utter publicly a two-syllable word: "Sorry." We also kept reminding people of how internationally prized traditional Aboriginal culture was, directing attention towards dance, paintings, the spiritual and intellectual sophistication of the "Dreaming". And we urged political action – walking across bridges, signing "sorry" books, because doing those things were signs, however inadequate, of the sincerity of our hearts.

They were good things to do, and I am sure my woman did them. But meanwhile other things were happening. She was hearing other stories, or fragments of stories; sometimes just snapshots of action. They came in the form of radio or newspaper reports from places with names she had never heard, and they told of the neglect or physical and sexual abuse of children, of the beating and killing of women, of plagues of adolescent suicides, of suicidal substance-abuse – alcohol, drugs, petrol and solvents, used as if there were no tomorrow. They came like lightning flashes illuminating a Boschian landscape we did not recognise at all.

There is a demoralising condition psychologists call "cognitive dissonance", when two incompatible ideas struggle to co-exist in one mind. I think we set my woman, and others like her, up for it. I had the sense right through that time that we were declaiming with our backs turned to the desperate, disintegrating societies behind us; in part because we were entranced by our own discourse; in part because we were persuaded it mattered; in part because we were stricken by what our flourishing had cost them; but perhaps most because we thought ourselves incompetent to understand why these things were happening, save in the broadest post-colonial theoretical terms – "dispossession", "impoverishment", "despair" – which generalities somehow failed to grip the realities of what we were looking at.

Criticism is easy, especially for someone whose preferred position is on the sidelines. So today, time willing, I want to look at three lightning-flash scenes; to try to hold the light steady, and to draw closer to what was going on. Not Redfern, because Redfern is a special urban case drenched with symbolic importance. (I'd refer you to Gillian Cowlishaw's work for refracted light on Redfern.) My focus will be on two fringe camps and one "remote community", because it is those kinds of settlements whites most readily think of when we think of "Aborigines" rather than the 70 per cent of people of Aboriginal descent who now live in the towns and cities, and because it is from places like these that the lightning-flash reports most often come.

First to push aside a couple of words which persistently block our attempts to grasp what is going on, beginning with the word "community". "Community". In our culture it generates a rosy glow, conjuring a cluster of families spilling in and out of each other's houses, looking after each other's kids, sharing values: a little commonwealth.

Aboriginal "communities" are not like that. Most began as arbitrary agglomerations of tribes, often hostile to each other, rounded up and dumped down to live cheek-by-jowl on alien land, or, worse, on land belonging to one group, so the interlopers were condemned to a chronic state of trespass, and the traditional owners to chronic grievance. Even where a people were settled on their own land, the very process of settling deformed traditional practices, and therefore traditional relationships. And if "Community" evokes for us notions of fluent egalitarianism, in most Aboriginal "communities" family remains the primary, visceral loyalty, and a major stumbling block in the way of our democratic schemes for their improvement.

However, it is also true, as I hope to show, that some of these artificial agglomerations have been forged on the anvil of "the colonial experience" into true communities, Aboriginal-style.

So ... we need permanent inverted commas around that word "community". In every case, we will have to establish just what it means.

The second word is "culture". That is a vast issue which (like everything else in this rough sketch of a lecture) I am pursuing elsewhere. For the moment: when we speak of "traditional Aboriginal culture", we either think in "high-culture" terms of dance, visual arts and so on, or, if our usage is slightly more anthropologised, we evoke a vision of a "sharing" culture, which in these new-age days slides easily towards a notion of a "caring" culture. We need to remember that "sharing cultures" are moral economies designed to manage scarcity. Of necessity, they are tough on their members. And if you must share with some, you must not share with others.

I will be using the word "culture" to mean the system of meanings which sustains a particular group at a particular time regarding their expectations of themselves and each other: to quote myself, the last resort of the depleted: "a dynamic system of shared meanings through which we communicate with our own."

Because cultural meanings are rarely made explicit, understanding another culture's meanings is and always will be a hazardous enterprise. There is a sentimental notion abroad that we humans, skin-colour and costume aside, are the same under the skin. I blame it on that 1950s collection of photographs titled *The Family of Man* – gorgeous babies, grinning ancients, heart-stoppingly beautiful children, great hats, and that cute Peruvian boy playing the flute on the cover. It found its way into every household, even ours. But it isn't true. We are not the same. We are different. That is our burden, and our glory.

For me, the most compelling theme in our multi-level national history is our failure to grasp the continuing cultural differences between the descendants of the original Australians and the rest of us.

The first lightning flash illuminates one such difference: what can look to us to be a terrifying Aboriginal propensity for unembarrassed, public, verbal and/or physical violence.

Just as each culture has its own concept of what constitutes masculine courage or feminine grace, so each culture is differently habituated to inflicting and enduring violence. Most of us have not suffered physical assault since primary school. When we see public violence it is usually decently clad in the brief garments of sport. When it is not, we call the cops to do the authorised violence necessary to stop it.

In *Dancing with Strangers* I counter-poised what the British saw as wild, out-of-control Aboriginal violence – bashings, spearings, all-in battles – against what Aboriginal Australians saw as wild, out-of-control British violence – hangings, shacklings, floggings. Each culture drew its own lines to separate socially sanctioned from unauthorised, illegal violence. Drawing the lines so differently, they persistently got each other wrong, as when Phillip fetched up getting himself speared at what he thought was a reconciliation party. (Which, indeed, it was, in its way.)

David Collins, Judge Advocate to the new colony and therefore a man with a professional interest in keeping the King's peace, spotted the intercultural problem early:

> An inhabitant of Port Jackson is seldom seen, even in the populous town of Sydney, without his spear, his throwing-stick, or his club. His spear is his defence against enemies. It is the weapon which he uses to punish aggression and revenge insult. It is even the instrument with which he corrects his wife in the last extreme; for in their passion, or perhaps oftener in a fit of jealousy, they scruple not to inflict death ...

> It is easy to perceive what effect this must have upon their minds.
> They become familiarised to wounds, blood, and death; and, repeat-
> edly involved in skirmishes and dangers, the native fears not death
> in his own person, and is consequently careless of inflicting it on
> others. [Collins, *Account of the English Colony in New South Wales*, 2, p.182]

For an Aboriginal man at the time of contact, the initial defence of
rights and enforcement of law lay with his own person. That cultural
understanding was to have large consequences on ongoing social relations
between black and white.

I offer one violent moment from a post-colonial Aboriginal community, this one remarkable because it was created not by whites but
independently, indeed illegally, by Aborigines: the Darwin fringe-camp
Basil Sansom immortalised as *The Camp at Wallaby Cross*. Aboriginal entrepreneurs developed the camp as a safe house for Aboriginal stockmen
and mission people come to the city to drink their accumulated pay or
pension-cheques. It functioned as a hostel for binge-drinkers on a base of
more permanent members-by-choice. Sansom is my kind of anthropologist because he pulls us into close-up on a particular incident, and then
tries to work out what is going on. From his marvellous book I choose
one event. And yes, I know the dangers of misuse of material like this.

The Scene. It is late morning. We are inside the camp. A big man,
100-plus kilos, is beating a woman, his current wife, before a large group
of people, who are watching but making no attempt to intervene. The
woman lies on the ground, unresisting; he is hitting her with a metre-long
piece of wood, he is shouting abuse as he hits her. He hits her eight times,
walks away, while he continues to proclaim his grievances. He has been
drinking, but he is not drunk. The man's daughter attacks the woman,
pummelling her; the woman moans; the man comes back, kicks her in
the face four times, walks away still shouting; the girl pummels the
woman again. Then the man picks up an axe, a woman in the crowd calls
imperiously for him to put it down, he does so, walks away; the daughter

pummels the woman, walks away; the woman lies sobbing; the watching people disperse. It is over. [Sansom, *The Camp at Wallaby Cross*, pp.92–5 – but you will need to read all of Chapter 4 to appreciate the movement of the argument.]

This scene has a special interest for me because it exactly echoes the scene Baneelon staged before Governor Phillip when, after publicly proclaiming both his grievances and his murderous intentions (thus collecting an anxious cloud of British witnesses), he snatched up a weapon and attacked a young woman who made not the least attempt to protect herself, before a group of silent watchers who made no attempt to intervene. And when Phillip's men grabbed him, Baneelon was ecstatic with rage. [Clendinnen, *Dancing with Strangers*, pp.144–51]

Phillip was disgusted by what was done that day, and so are we with this. Nonetheless, and exactly because our cherished cultural values are so directly outraged – large man beating small woman, violence inflicted on an unresisting victim, no intervention from onlookers – it is essential that we understand what is happening from the participants' point of view. Sansom diagnosed the scene as an act of moral violence: in other words, of authorised justice, with the grievance publicly proclaimed, the punishment publicly inflicted, and then publicly terminated: when the man picks up the axe the watching woman calls in effect "Hold! Enough!" – and he stops. If he hadn't, Sansom believes that silent audience – that comprehensive jury – would have intervened.

Furthermore, had the man been drunk, the people of the drinkers' camp at Wallaby Cross would have intervened earlier. There seems to have been a general view among Aborigines (a view now changing) that drunks aren't responsible for what they do – a belief which seethes with uncomfortable implications. However, one implication is that you can't do justice when you are drunk.

Therefore there is in my view no continuity between the socially controlled moral violence we have just been watching and the individual, uncontrolled, sometimes lethal violence we see in many Aboriginal communities today, most often inflicted by drunken men on women – with the "community" (remember those quotation marks) too exhausted to intervene.

The camp at Wallaby Cross impresses me as a remarkable post-colonial Aboriginal creation: a community, without the quotation marks, built out of the radical displacement and radical mixing of tribal groups. The camp also tamed that flamboyantly destructive introduced element, alcohol. The people at Wallaby Cross, drinkers themselves, held alcohol's potential to dissolve social bonds in check, and they did it on territory reconquered from the colonisers, or, more precisely, from the Darwin municipal council. The camp's enduring raison d'être was to exist free from white control, while still enjoying the white man's irresistible gifts of alcohol, radios, guitars, flash stockmen's gear, store provisions, tobacco, grog. Sansom's tight focus on the particular and the actual lets us look deeper, past that initial shudder, to an unfamiliar form of community.

Wallaby Cross, this brilliant evolution from "tradition", depended on a small but secure economic base. Bonus capital was injected into the community from outsiders' pay cheques, but its stability depended on the judicious deployment of the government pensions regularly paid to the old, to widows, and to mothers receiving child support. The recipients handed over their cheques to the camp organisers, its *de facto* elders, in return for protection, security and prestige; and these elders of an invented community organised corroborees, even initiations out of their (highly irregular) use of government funding.

I don't know what happened when unemployment benefits came in. My guess is that the uncontrolled inflow of money to the young and strong would disrupt a moral economy based on the controlled redistribution of scarce resources. An experiment in social adaptation destroyed by benevolent intervention.

Another glimpse of a post-colonial agglomeration of indigenous people responding creatively to the devastations attending the white man's coming: this time the Waramungu from around Tennant Creek.

They had had a hard time of it. Pastoralists had been thrusting into their arid country from the turn of the century, with all the usual brutalities. Then in 1934 gold was discovered, and in came the miners. A young anthropologist named Bill Stanner happened to be in the vicinity and describes the brand of European Civilisation the Waramungu had to face:

> a stretch of bush pockmarked with scattered shafts ... little food, less water, almost no ready money; rough humpies and scores of hard customers with that worst of fevers, gold fever. I had to keep a gun hard by to guard my stores. [Stanner, *After the Dreaming*, pp.15–16]

Stanner heard talk of the need to clear the remaining Aborigines out of the way to a stretch of bad country where he himself had almost died from lack of water, despite having local guides. He reported what was being planned to the only authorities he knew in those days: his Research Council. Without result: as he says, with typical Stanneresque economy, "the miners won and the Warumungu lost." And Tennant Creek was born.

There is an alternative myth to explain this miraculous blossoming of a town in the middle of a desert. En route to elsewhere a beer truck had broken down; people came from nowhere and camped beside it, and presto! Tennant Creek, born like Aphrodite from the foam. From its beginning, Tennant Creek was a town of gargantuan drinkers.

The white town grew with the usual fringe of displaced Aborigines living in squalid camps around it: camps which C.D. Rowley described in the late '60s as "among the worst on the continent". Some families were still living on their home country as (largely unpaid) workers on cattle leases. Some came into town when the federal government began paying old-age and widow's pensions in the late '50s, because those small payments opened a small window of choice. The rest were abruptly tipped off their lands in the early '70s when equal pay for black and white stockmen came in: a decision taken elsewhere, for the usual mixed motives, and, of course, with no consultation of the people most affected. Who crammed into the town camps too. Where else could they go? Soon there were ten camps, with sixteen different language groups piled into them. The Waramungu had been very thoroughly processed by "the colonial process".

Meanwhile ... Tennant Creek was becoming famous for its wild Aboriginal drinkers, providing quite a few lightning flashes to astonish white Australia.

Then in the mid-'80s, something remarkable happened. A representative council emerged from those camps, we don't know how, because it happened spontaneously, out of white sight. Julalikari Council included all the camps and all the language groups, so breaking free from the crippling constrictions of clan and family loyalties and the conflicting traditional ownerships which still bedevil Aboriginal politics today. Its single purpose was to fight the effects of grog on the people.

Tennant Creek, population 60 per cent white, 40 per cent black, was as I say famous for its night scenes of drunken Aborigines surging out of the liquor outlets, brawling up and down the main street, smashing expensive windows, fighting, bleeding, sometimes dying on the pavements. So the Council organised a Night Patrol. Unpaid volunteers, most of them senior people, many of them women, all of them non-drinkers, would go out at night in pairs, in a van or more often on foot, to collect drunks and to break up trouble before it could explode into violence. Some senior members were putting in thirty hours a week on top of their daily work. The Council also staged "morning-after" petty sessions in the different camps. Men who would take on white police without thinking twice blenched when they had to face the anger of the kin and neighbours they had monstered the night before. And note the innovation. These drunks were being held responsible for their action, and their families would not protect them from the formidable community punishment of public shaming.

Meanwhile ... the meat-works and the mine had closed, white Tennant Creek had fallen on hard times, and local businessmen were dreaming of a tourist-led recovery. They certainly didn't want those phantom tourists frightened off by mobs of all-too-real drunken Aborigines. So, in March

1994, they called a "summit" on grog, with the title making their priorities plain: "Tennant Creek, Tourism and Grog".

Meanwhile … Julalikari Council had been carrying its analysis further, from issues of misuse to issues of supply. Camps which had proclaimed themselves "dry" were still being ringed by binge drinkers, with the drunks bringing their violence and their rage back into the home camp when the grog ran out.

So at that first summit meeting, the Julalikari Council moved to restrict the availability of alcohol in Tennant Creek, which is possible under Northern Territory law. They wanted a grog-free day (Thursday, which was pension-day), and for the rest of the week pub and takeaway hours to be restricted to from noon to 8 p.m., with takeaways limited to six cans per person and the sale of wine casks prohibited altogether. And (here comes the rub) they wanted those restrictions to apply to the whole community of Tennant Creek, black and white alike. They wanted a social – indeed, given the power relations in the town, a political – revolution.

What happened next is told in a book written by Alexis Wright, an Aboriginal woman from the Gulf country called in by the Council to write the history of the struggle. She calls her book *Grog War*, because that is what it was. Initially it is a difficult book to read, because Wright uses a kind of hand-held camera technique for reporting the two-year-long round of meetings between the Julalikari Council and the liquor interests before the Northern Territory Liquor Commission, with the rest of the town lined up barracking.

There were some interesting re-alignments. Aboriginal and white drinkers united in opposition to the Council. So did Aboriginal and white progressives, taking the right to drink as emblematic of Aboriginal enfranchisement. White Territorians knew it was their basic human right to drink what, when and where they chose. After all, it wasn't their fault that Abos couldn't handle the grog. The solution was easy. Let the blackfellas buy whatever grog they wanted as takeaway and go back to the camps to drink it, just as they used to in the good old days of *de facto* curfew.

Meanwhile ... the publicans were playing a seriously hard game suffused by a deep moral flush in defence of individual rights and legitimate commercial interests. They were defending life, liberty and the pursuit of profits. They said that as liquor sellers they had the right and the duty to provide a service and to profit from uncoerced commercial transactions, and these transactions were certainly uncoerced: they themselves had proved Aborigines were so desperate to buy they would buy under any conditions. They were also aggrieved by the necessity of competing with their fellow-publicans for what threatened to be a diminished trade. That was anti-mate, anti-social and anti-Australian. As for the rest – once the Abos were out of the pub they weren't their problem. That was for the police, or the Night Patrol, or the government. Or someone.

Race relations in the town, always bad, were now vicious, so the Liquor Commissioner offered a concession: he was ready to introduce a special measure to the *Anti-Discrimination Act* and to restrict the availability of alcohol to Tennant Creek's Aborigines. The Council refused. Bloody-minded? You bet. Why not, after their history?

But there was a lot more than bloody-mindedness going on here. An expanded sense of community was struggling to be born in a deeply, casually hostile environment. This is when Wright's close reporting of apparently futile exchanges matters. We watch as people wearily trade the same old slogans like punches; as these two people, forced by history to live in proximity, find new ways to vex each other. (Each side loathed the other's conduct in court.) And as we listen, we identify a language problem. Both sides were using the same words, but each meant different things by them.

When the Julalikari Council people talked about "the community", they meant "all of the people living in this place". Country, language, tribe had been remorselessly taken from them, so now they were making a new community out of what they had. They had consistently refused to abandon their own disruptive drinkers to some netherworld of despair and rejection. Instead, night after night, through the years, they had gone out to gather them up, and bring them home. They had cared for some old white people camped near them in exactly the same way.

They also knew the tight nexus between the ruthless financial interests of white suppliers, and the costs of alcohol dependence. They knew that down to the last bruised woman, the last hungry child. They also knew that when whites started talking about their "rights", Aborigines would do well to watch their backs.

Grog War holds up a mirror in which we see reflected the Aboriginal experience of us. Reading it, I felt the terrible justice of the judgement on whites made to Bill Stanner by an old Aboriginal man after years spent trying to co-exist civilly with us: "Very clever people; very hard people; plenty humbug."

That is not the way we look to ourselves. I think it is often the way we still can look to them, however virtuous our intentions, however elevated our rhetoric – indeed, because of its very elevation.

So what happened? After two years of talk and trials of different kinds of restrictions, the Council got most of what they wanted. The Town Council, which had previously opposed them, moved sleekly to take the credit, another familiar white strategy. And the majority of white residents, along with the majority of black residents, applauded the victory. Their town was now a better place to live. The Council's obstinacy had created a community which had not existed before: a community which tran-scended race boundaries. There was still division, but now it ran between irresponsible drinkers and suppliers, black and white – the publicans and the sinners – and the rest of the citizenry, white and black.

Of course it is not all roses. The obsessive drinking continues, though it is rather more orderly. The police and the Council work together well. There is what one of the Council warriors, a remarkable man called Dave Curtis (look him up on the internet) calls "a modicum of racial harmony" where there had been none before. In this war the victories are small, and always precarious.

My last lightning flash comes from a place called Curtin Springs, on the Lasseter Highway about 100 kilometres east of Uluru. There is a road-house there. (You can look that up on the internet, too.) It was opened in 1964 by a pastoralist who had taken up his lease only four years before, and who wanted to expand his meagre income by serving tourists on the thirsty drive to Uluru tourist country. His application for a liquor licence was passionately opposed by the three Aboriginal communities in the region, all of them, although officially "dry", beset by alcohol, but the licence was granted anyway. The licensee, who was not a bad fellow, nonetheless arrived at a gentleman's agreement. All drinking would be done on the premises. There would be no takeaway sales. Then in 1988, with his income shrinking as tourism dropped off, he began to exercise his legal right to sell takeaway alcohol to Aborigines. He did, however, limit the sales: only one carton of beer and one four-litre wine cask per person per day. The young men would come in from the settlements, drink, and then take themselves, their supplies and their drunkenness back to their "dry" communities, and turn them into nightmares. ("Very clever people; very hard people; plenty humbug.")

So the women of the besieged communities organised, withdrawing consent both from their traditional powerlessness and from the power-lessness imposed on them by white authorities. They fought with new weapons, holding public meetings; marching, painted and with ban-ners, down empty roads with the cameras pre-arranged. And they talked, loud and clear, in public, like this Anangu woman before the Liquor Commissioner: "We have been asking for years and years to close Curtin Springs down. I ask you, could you not listen to us for once? We have lost a lot of our lads to drinking. We are not going to cry all the time."

They were reminded that as citizens, Aborigines had an equal right with whites to drink. But they were speaking out of a concept of rights which went beyond the individual, and they had the dreadful weight of experience behind them. So the Curtin Springs women reached past the local and deeper into the public sphere. They went after a "special measure" exemption from the *Anti-Discrimination Act*, and finally they got it (after, may I say, a woman commissioner had come into office). The roadhouse-keeper was forbidden to sell takeaway liquor to Anangu people.

Of course the destabilising thrusts have kept coming. Right now those same Anangu communities are tottering under a great upsurge in petrol-sniffing. Further south, Bob Collins has just taken over the administration of Anangu-Pitjantjatjara lands, in response to a plea from the women, to try to get some action to combat it. Petrol-sniffing is also resurgent among white kids in the Northern Territory, perhaps because they are realising they have almost no choices, either.

As for my conclusions: just as the three men in Sydney said, I think we must wait on local Aboriginal initiatives, because only local Aboriginal initiatives are sufficiently informed by local knowledge of the particular historical experience and the particular balance of pressures and person-alities in a particular place, at a particular time.

We will find the waiting hard. Like Amanda Vanstone, we ("naturally", culturally) favour clean, across-the-board solutions, and like Amanda Vanstone, we have a mighty urge to intervene. I think Aboriginal Australia has suffered enough from our impatient, ignorant, or careless interven-tions (the families tumbled off their country when equal wages came in; Wallaby Cross with unemployment relief disrupting that unique, deli-cately calibrated moral economy).

We will have to learn to practise an unfamiliar virtue: to tolerate uncer-tainty. Understanding a profoundly different culture is a slow business, especially given the mistrust generated by a history of systematic injustice. It will be a slow road to enlightenment, with those "Ah! Now I see!" moments mere stations along the way.

We can no longer depend on a mix of sound-bite compilations and moral intuitions to form our judgements, nor the brief but blinding illuminations of lightning flashes, either. We need good, up-close, non-ideologised anthropologies of particular places or the evolution of par-ticular problems traced through time. There is already an abundance of marvellous studies buried in academic archives, like Maggie Brady's analysis of petrol-sniffing, now a decade old, still utterly relevant, or David McKnight's angry, loving, informed account of what has happened from settlement to now on Mornington Island. I was surprised by the richness, once I got past the ideologised crust.

I think at least one part of our ill-defined job ought to be to exhume some of those analyses and report them to the general public: to help them understand why particular communities have been brought to the pass they are in, so their plight becomes humanly intelligible to us, and not some blank crime of man or nature. We can't expect journalists to do that. Their concern has to be with the lightning-flash "now". We can't expect the researchers to do it, either. They have to report to their departmental employers, or to their peers, so their work will typically need some translation for a general readership.

We will also have to decide to which voices we will listen, when there are so many voices, some opportunistic, some ideologised beyond recovery, some embittered beyond recall. As with any society, I think we will listen to the voices which command our respect: where we hear the depth of experience and the intrepid reasoning informing speech and actions. I hear those qualities in Noel Pearson's voice: Pearson, whose intelligence and natural eloquence would have given him a national career, but who chose to turn back to his own Cape York mob, and to work for them; Pearson, who knows the odds. A few years ago he gave himself a fifty-fifty chance of doing what he knows what must be done, if destruction is to be averted. I also listen to Pearson because he makes me recognise my own areas of cultural blindnesses. These days I find myself coming to agree with him where I had disagreed before. I listen to Bob Collins, who happens to be white, because he, like Pearson, is locked into local circumstance; because, like Pearson, he is an effective hinge-man, responsive to local insights, yet capable of manipulating national authorities; and because his recognition of his moral duty goes beyond cultural difference to where our shared humanity resides.

And I will listen to the equivalents of Julalikari Council and of the women of Curtin Springs. Toni Morrison once explained her deep pleasure in Greek tragedy by its family resemblance to the fierce battles fought between the claims of the individual, the family and the community among disoriented Afro-Americans. The women at Curtin Springs were impelled by external forces quite beyond their control to make a Sophoclean choice: to jeopardise the lives of their beloved sons, husbands, brothers – to condemn them to the long, dangerous drive to Alice Springs to get the grog they could not live without; to be alone in Alice, beyond the loving protection of their kin – to preserve the rest of their community. Any culture must honour the terrible clear-sightedness of that choice – and that they should have had the courage to discover choice in that apparently sealed and hopeless, externally contrived situation.

Alexis Wright used this quote from a white resident of Tennant Creek as the epigraph for her *Grog War*: "I know what Aboriginal people do because I watch them from the top of the hill."

We will need to draw much closer than that.

Addendum

After the lecture I was asked – very reasonably, given my emphasis on the local – what writings I had found most useful on Victorian Aborigines. At the time I couldn't answer. When I looked my mind was bare, which can happen after a lecture. Now, restored, I would say the books which most enlightened me have been Diane Barwick's *Rebellion at Corranderk*; Don Watson's *Caledonia Australis*, on Gippsland; Bain Attwood's *The Making of the Aborigines*, on the Lake Tyers district; and, above all, the journals of George Augustus Robinson and the Reverend William Thomas (who took over as Protector from Robinson), published by the Victorian Archaeological Survey (for my account of Robinson, see "Reading Mr. Robinson", in *Tiger's Eye*).

Main references

Brady, Maggie, *Heavy Metal: The Social Meaning of Petrol Sniffing in Australia*, Aboriginal Studies Press, Canberra, 1992.

Sansom, Basil, *The Camp at Wallaby Cross: Aboriginal Fringe-Dwellers in Darwin*, Australian Institute of Aboriginal Studies, Darwin, 1980.

Wright, Alexis, *Grog War*, Magabala Books Aboriginal Corporation, Broome, 1997.

Additional references

On public punishment and expressive violence:

Langton, Marcia, "Medicine Square", in *Being Black: Aboriginal Culture in "Settled" Australia*, Ian Keen (ed.), Aboriginal Studies Press, Canberra, [1988] 1991.

Cowlishaw, Gillian, *Blackfellas, Whitefellas, and the Hidden Injuries of Race*, Blackwell, Malden, Mass., 2004.

On Mornington Island:

McKnight, David, "Fighting in an Aboriginal Supercamp", in David Riches (ed.), *The Anthropology of Violence*, Blackwell, Oxford and New York, 1986; and his *From Hunting to Drinking: The Devastating Effects of Alcohol on an Australian Aboriginal Community*, Routledge, London, 2002.

See also Dick Roughsey (Goobalathaldin), *Moon and Rainbow*, Rigby Limited, Adelaide, 1970, for an unabashed insider's view.

Anthony Bubalo

Perhaps the funniest line in Paul McGeough's essay on Iraq, Mission Impossible, comes towards the end. McGeough calls most of the 200-odd newspapers now published in Iraq "propaganda sheets that protect the vested interests of one political party or another rather than foster constructive debate". Not like in Australia right?

It's a cheap shot but there is a point. One senses from the essay that McGeough has genuine affection for the Iraqis he interviews and writes about. But there is also a hint of disappointment, even disdain. McGeough tells us we should not expect Iraqis to become democrats overnight (if at all), while at other times he holds Iraqis to an impossible standard, as in the reference above. It is as if he has a case of what a Palestinian friend used to call "Lawrence of Arabia syndrome"; that is, something of a love and a loathing of "the Arabs" all at the same time.

It is not, of course, an uncommon phenomenon if you spend time in the Middle East. You come to love the individuals and the exotic history, culture and politics of the countries you live in; you almost idealise it. But that which makes it exotic and attracts you also makes you despair of "the Arabs" ever modernising their economies or systems of government. It can even lead to branding as naive and inauthentic those individual Arabs you meet who seem to have "Western" aspirations. Today, more than ever, this disposition is unhelpful. It's time for us all to grow up and put Lawrence back on the bookshelf where he belongs.

This is not to dismiss what McGeough has attempted to do in his essay. He has ventured beyond the threshold of his Baghdad hotel to allow, as he puts it, "Iraqi voices to reveal why today's Iraq is not the nursery for democracy that Washington wants it to be". This is a lot more than many journalists have done and probably more than most Coalition officials. For this reason alone the essay deserves to be read carefully.

McGeough takes aim at the American project to stabilise and democratise Iraq (if indeed the latter is the American aim). It is hard to argue with the proposition that Washington has botched the peace in Iraq as spectacularly as it won the war. Moreover it seems valid to argue, as McGeough does, that the US could have made better use of Iraq's tribes to stabilise the country (not to mention the former Iraqi Army). As is abundantly clear, without short-term stability any effort at reconstruction or indeed democratisation will prove impossible.

But you have to have sympathy for the US military officer who complains to McGeough that if it were that simple, they would have done it; if nothing else the Americans are good at expediency. From the reports of other Iraq watchers, the US does in fact appear to be engaging the tribal system, if only belatedly, as McGeough acknowledges. I would imagine that one problem might be the long line of tribal sheikhs who will tell you (and the odd journalist) they can deliver security in a particular area – for a price, of course. The problem is that the Americans simply lack the local knowledge to know whom to believe.

The US also faces a conundrum that McGeough doesn't quite acknowledge. Using the tribes to restore security and end the insurgency, as McGeough seems to recommend, may serve the short-term goal of stability. But it will also make McGeough's prophecy of Iraq becoming "Beirut writ large" more likely by hampering the long-term effort to reinforce a national identity and create a political system which isn't entirely divided on confessional, ethnic or tribal lines. (By the way, Beirut isn't even like Beirut anymore and is now a reasonably good example of how a war-weary people can overcome confessional divisions.) In other words the Americans are damned if they do and damned if they don't.

Indeed, the fear is not that the US will ignore the tribes, but that it will empower them. In other words, that the US will go down the well-trodden path of expediency as it has elsewhere in the Middle East. The fact that the Arab countries embraced by the US are no more than "liberalised autocracies", as McGeough points out, is partly because in the past the US was never really interested in sacrificing its interests for the sake of pushing democratisation. But let's not be churlish. For years Australia was happy to live with an autocratic Indonesia, and the realists would argue quite rightly too. Pity the US, therefore, when it gets attacked for being a status quo power and still gets attacked when it suddenly becomes a revisionist one.

There is, however, something more fundamental about McGeough's essay that leaves me uneasy. In his rush to tell us why the US can't democratise Iraq, McGeough also dismisses too readily the ability of Iraqis themselves to democratise. He is clearly sensitive to this charge when he notes that it may be "politically incorrect, racist even, to question the ability or desire of Arabs to embrace democracy". It probably isn't racist, but I still think it is wrong-headed to portray democracy as something alien to Iraq, if not to the broader Middle East. It is not that far from the assumptions that underpin the neo-conservative argument that democracy needs to be imposed in the region.

It is time that we change the paradigm for talking about democracy in the Middle East. True enough, as McGeough notes, there aren't a lot of democratic countries in the region to cite as examples. But this does not mean that there aren't democratic aspirations. I agree with McGeough when he says that Washington's notion of Iraq as a democratic beachhead in the Middle East is flawed. Not because Iraq can't be democratic and therefore can't serve as an example, but because the citizens of the Middle East do not need an example.

Today democracy is not exclusively for the West to export or impose; it is a global commodity. It may take different forms and routes in different countries – it might not always be "Jeffersonian" – but in the end what underpins democracy is the desire of individuals to have a say in the way their lives are run. After successive centuries of imperial, colonial and autocratic rule, this is not a sentiment you need to export to the Middle East. In Iran today, students and reformists fight to expand political pluralism. In the Palestinian territories, efforts are being made to remove the dead hand of a decrepit leadership. In Egypt, reformist Islamists seek to register a political party and call for democratic elections. Even in Saudi Arabia, middle-class Saudis push quietly to make their government more transparent. Is Iraq really so different?

McGeough will no doubt argue that he is simply telling us what Iraqis themselves say. But which Iraqis? During his visit to Sydney this year, the Iraqi blogger Salam Pax said that in responding to foreigners' questions about Iraq he felt the tremendous pressure of being perceived to speak for all Iraqis. You wonder whether the Iraqis in McGeough's essay are able to bear a similar burden. McGeough says the more he talked to Iraqi tribal sheikhs, the more clearly he realised that "the most fundamental power structures in Iraqi society run counter to those which underpin democracy". Certainly his essay leaves little doubt that these tribal leaders are, if nothing else, self-serving. You wonder, therefore, why Iraqi sheikhs would give McGeough any other impression.

It is true that McGeough didn't talk only to tribal leaders. But you are still left with the feeling that the sample is a little too convenient to the argument. It would have been nice to have heard from more Iraqis like those he interviewed who worked as translators for the Coalition, who tell us about their hopes for an Iraq with American colleges, an American justice system and American amusement arcades. McGeough applauds them for their bravery as quickly as he condemns them for their naivety; love and loathing again. Perhaps, as his limited sampling implies, there aren't too many like them. But given that some 75 per cent of Iraqis are urbanised and 50 per cent of the population are under twenty, I have my doubts.

McGeough describes tribalism as the "bedrock under the bedrock" of Iraqi society. But another way to view tribalism is as a societal default. That is, in the absence of national and institutional alternatives, Iraqis fall back on tribal connections to settle their conflicts, represent their interests and provide them with protection. Looked at in this way, Iraqi tribalism is less an obstacle to change than something whose influence has ebbed and flowed throughout Iraq's history. This is not to say that tribalism and religion are not significant factors in Iraqi or indeed Middle Eastern politics; quite clearly they are. But McGeough seems to leave little scope for evolution, for adaptation or for competing influences in his conception of the way Iraqi society operates.

Unlike McGeough I haven't visited Iraq, so the best I can do is reach for a history book. In it you find a more complex and evolving picture of tribalism than McGeough's snapshot presents. In the nineteenth century, for example, Ottoman economic and political reform diluted tribal power to the point where, according to Dr Faleh Jabar, an Iraqi sociologist, Ottoman Iraq became known as the "graveyard of the tribes". Central administration, fast and reliable communications, and the re-organisation of land tenure all served to undercut tribalism to the point where some tribes and tribal confederations disappeared altogether.

One also finds this complex picture under Iraq's relatively short-lived experience of parliamentary democracy during the Hashemite Monarchy's rule from 1921 to 1958. As the American anthropologist Robert Fernea noted, the Iraqi tribal community in which he lived from 1956 to 1958 saw a struggle between two ways of organising life, that of the state and that of the tribe, and it wasn't always the tribe that came out on top. Indeed, what destroyed the nascent and admittedly imperfect institutions of political representation in the 1950s was not tribalism, but autocracy. The regime's destruction of civil and state institutions left people with little option but to seek refuge in traditional ones.

In place of McGeough's image of the timeless power of the tribe, therefore, you get a more complex picture of tribes and tribal confederations that break up, disappear, are eclipsed and re-form and – most importantly – are manipulated by a succession of rulers from the British to Saddam. It is why Iraq experts today speak of a society that has been "re-tribalised". The irony is that even Saddam came ultimately to rely on the same societal default, as McGeough notes. This was not because of the strength or cohesiveness of the tribes, but precisely because they could be bought off and played off against each other and represented much less of a threat to him than an Army general. Later it would be because the Army had been weakened by the first two Gulf wars. In both cases, however, tribalism was less the cause of state failure than a symptom of it.

Perhaps what McGeough is really pointing to is the persistence of a tribal ethos or, as he puts it, of a society that is "top-down driven". This is what is called the "culturalist" approach to the Middle East that argues there is something in Arab culture that makes the region more prone to dictatorships because "the Arabs" appreciate strong leaders. Let's assume for a moment that this isn't a caricature. Isn't it possible to want strong leaders and at the same time to appreciate the ability to choose the strong leader you want? Indeed, in tribal societies throughout the Middle East, being "born to rule" is only half the story. The fact that sons and brothers are often passed over when it comes time to choose a new tribal leader underlines the extent to which fitness to rule and consensus are also important parts of this ethos.

Similarly we often make the assumption in the West that secularism is necessary for democracy. Yet the vast majority of the Middle East's autocrats are secular, and many of those pushing for democratic change are Islamists. In Iraq McGeough hints that the growing power of Grand Ayatollah al-Sistani may portend a theocracy along Iranian lines. He is right when he says that no one really knows what Sistani thinks. So why assume that he would adopt an Iranian theocratic model that to this day stands outside Shiite orthodoxy? Were this Sistani's goal he could very easily have backed Moqtada al-Sadr's uprising rather than being the critical figure in snuffing it out. Indeed, his actions to date seem more consistent with a hard-headed calculation that some form of representational government will finally give the Shiite majority a say in running the country.

None of the above should be taken to suggest that I believe Iraq is inevitably on a democratic trajectory. In many respects it is too early to tell. What my argument is really aimed at is changing the terms of the debate. Whatever its motivations, the US removed Saddam. You could even argue there was some justice in the US expending political, financial and human capital to remove a regime it had once supported with disastrous consequences for ordinary Iraqis (and even perhaps that the US is learning a valuable lesson in imperial overreach). But what we need to understand is that what happens next in Iraq will depend not on the US, but, quite rightly, on Iraqis themselves.

Anthony Bubalo

Paul McGeough

Amman, 1 August: The reason for writing about the tribes is that they are virtually ignored by those with their hands on the levers of power in post-war Iraq and they get scant attention from the international media. Yet, as a crucial power-base they need to be understood and reckoned with if the new Iraq is to find the kind of peace and security in which a new nation might be built. Anthony Bubalo is right when he says that the Americans are "damned if they do and damned if they don't" – the pity is that despite its huge resources, the US didn't take this into account in its planning for the aftermath of invasion. The tribes and the mosques were the only institutional forces left standing by the Americans – they disbanded the country's military; they left in tatters its bureaucracy, legal system and economy; and all members of the Baath Party, no matter how useful their skills might be, were drummed out of government positions. As the US still grapples with the hostility of the reception it received across Iraq, the result, notwithstanding the appointment of the Allawi interim government, is a power vacuum in which the tribes and the mosques have had a head-start to reassert themselves.

Bringing the tribes into the nation-rebuilding process would empower them, but leaving them out runs the risk of empowering them even more – as we are seeing. Bubalo presumes that the tribes might have only a negative impact on the new Iraq, but many of my interviews have revealed just how welcoming the tribes were towards the US, confirming a substantial reservoir of goodwill that the Americans might have exploited, even if the outcome was to be a "peculiarly Iraqi solution", to borrow the words used by the US military chief, Lieutenant General Ricardo Sanchez, when he speculated on the likely outcome of efforts to defuse the US clash with the renegade Shiite leader Moqtada al-Sadr in April this year. This is a region in which the tribes still have a significant say in how countries are run. To varying degrees, all the regimes here are autocratic, but unless the sheikhs bless the autocrat, the regime can run into serious difficulty.

It's worth noting that in Jordan the late King Hussein was masterful in his recognition and inclusion of the tribes; but his successor, the young King Abdullah II, doesn't have the same finesse. Now there are mutterings among the Jordanian sheikhs.

I'm writing from Amman, where analysts tell me that last week's demonstration by the Adwan tribe – in which tribesmen rallied outside a company's Amman office, warning that they would behead its executives unless the company abandoned its contracts in Iraq as demanded by Iraqi hostage-takers – was as much a protest at the new king's failure to deal with the tribes as it was a pragmatic tribal response to the imminent death of two of their tribesmen. It is a measure of the power of the Adwan, angered at their exclusion from Jordan's by-regal-appointment-only senate, that the company took only forty minutes to comply with the tribe's demand. Equally, in the impoverished south of Jordan, there are fears that the king's neglect of the tribes is making them more tolerant, if not welcoming, of al-Qaeda operatives and their associates seeking refuge from neighbouring Saudi Arabia.

Bubalo misses the point altogether when he quotes Dr Faleh Jabar on Ottoman Iraq being the "graveyard of the tribes" and Robert Fernea on the difficulties the tribes have faced under autocratic regimes. The reality is that they still exist as a force and, as they are demonstrating today, they have survived the greatest autocrat of modern Iraq – Saddam. Sounds like bedrock to me. Bubalo's four-word quote from Jabar may do the Iraqi sociologist a disservice, if the content of a collection he edited in 2002 is any guide. I'm on assignment and I don't have access to the book, but I've been able to read the on-line publisher's review of *Tribes and Power: Nationalism and Ethnicity in the Middle East* (Saqi Books, 2002) which gives a different take altogether on where Jabar sits in this debate. It's worth quoting:

> The advance of centralized polities, modern technology and the market economy, among other reasons, have clearly modified the tribe – sometimes beyond recognition. But tribes are not "passive" entities, for they have a life of their own; they flexibly mutate, producing various new forms of tribalism in the process and providing a platform for social, economic and political action. This platform has been allowed to expand and become more complex, despite the fact that authoritarian regimes have attempted to co-opt tribes through control and coercion. Nobility of lineage, tribal allegiance and other aspects of tribalism have been reactivated or restructured

to replace an eroded "modern" revolutionary legitimacy. The "new" tribes are politically savvy, adaptable and capable of playing for power.

Yesterday I dined with tribal elders in an ancient castle at Karak, high above the Dead Sea in the south of Jordan, and in keeping with the definition of contemporary tribes above, their preoccupation was how to extract money from the Jordanian government for a sound-and-light show and other crowd-pleasers for the remote castle. Most tour guides refer to this imposing fortress as a "Crusader" castle, but my host called it "Saladin's" castle. His point was that it was the Arab warrior Saladin who drove out the Crusaders. Over a traditional mensaf lunch, this sheikh of the Majali tribe explained that the tribes of Karak predated all the foreign forces that had occupied the city and its citadel – from the ancient Natabeans to the more recent twelfth-century arrival of the Crusaders and, later, the Mamluks and the British – and that the tribes were still a force to be reckoned with. The Ottomans had executed three of his forefathers in the castle; and, after lunch, he showed me the jailhouse in which he himself had been imprisoned briefly. With an air that bordered on smugness, he told me, "We are eating in the same place where Saladin ate." Yes, he said, there was an elected city council in Karak; but it was dominated by the tribes. He acknowledged that in Jordan there were two codes of law – tribal and notionally democratic – but added: "The way it works, is that as long as we can resolve issues according to tribal law, the government is happy to leave us to our own devices."

It would be dangerous to get too carried away with the romance of Lawrence of Arabia. But putting him back on the bookcase, as Bubalo urges, would be more dangerous. The reason for invoking his spirit is not to invoke David Lean hoopla so much as T.E. Lawrence's tenacious demonstration that a foreigner could work with the Arab tribes and, more importantly, that the tribes could agree to work with a foreigner. Today's Iraqi sheikhs complain bitterly about the inability of the US to treat them in accordance with their elaborate sense of dignity and respect. But Lawrence, in the words of an analyst here, "wore our clothes, sat on the floor with us, ate our food and learnt our language". John Negroponte, the new US Ambassador in Baghdad, doesn't have to go that far, and neither should he concede on every tribal demand, but he and the Allawi interim government do have to deal them in.

When King Hussein introduced what passes for democracy in Jordan in 1989, the first reaction of the sheikhs was that they did not want it because the appointment of a prime minister and a cabinet would reduce their access to the king. Their argument was that they already had a voice in a system in which the king had taken responsibility for everything, so why should they have to be responsible through the ballot box. Jordan now operates with system of government that, at best, might be described as a stepping-stone towards democracy – its senate and prime minister are appointed by the king, the cabinet is appointed by the prime minister and it has an ineffectual elected lower house, none of whose members can serve as prime minister or as members of the cabinet. Iraq had a similar arrangement under its British-appointed monarchy.

Bubalo is welcome to suggest that "we change the paradigm". He acknowledges that there is little democracy in the Middle East and that the Washington notion of a "democratic beachhead" in the region is flawed, and he pleads for the desire of individuals "to have their say". But the US has demonstrated a failure to understand the realpolitik of the existing paradigm, which leaves it in the same position as the American who, in the Irish joke, asks for directions to the post office – "Oh, I wouldn't start here …" his Dublin friend tells him. Indeed, as Bubalo says, there are nascent democratic stirrings in Iran and in Saudi Arabia. The activists behind these stirrings have a huge struggle ahead of them, but they are locally driven and they do not suffer from the handicap of their Iraqi counterparts – attempting to put down roots in the face of a much-loathed foreign occupation. Bubalo argues that historically "tribalism was less the cause of state failure …" – but to the extent that regimes in the region succeed, the tribes have been a reason for their survival.

He trots out the latest Iraq slogan from the US: "what happens next in Iraq will depend not on the US, but, quite rightly, on Iraqis themselves." But it is naive to assume that the US no longer exercises great power in Iraq or that it bears no responsibility for what unfolds, or that it is not attempting to shape the outcome. Its power is inordinate – it still has 150,000 troops in the country, and just who it allows to come to the table, by the application of its military, diplomatic and financial clout, will have a huge bearing on how Iraqis decide their fate and the extent of their pain and suffering along the way.

Likewise, his talk of "love and loathing" of the Arabs is a nonsense. My comments on the Baghdad press were intended not so much to denounce them as to remark on former US administrator Paul Bremer's habit of referring to their existence as proof of democracy at work. But the truth of the new Iraqi media is that as hostages to the narrow agenda of one party or another, they fail as tools of democracy. And for all the shortcomings of the Western press, it is absurd to compare them to the Iraqi media.

A more useful comparison with the West would examine the role of vested interests in politics. Bubalo is correct to note the self-serving nature of the tribes, but he doesn't take the next step – if the tribes have a power-base in Iraqi society, it would be foolhardy not to acknowledge them, in the same way that any significant and self-serving power-base would be acknowledged in the West. I have no antipathy for the good intentions of the many Iraqis who have unquestionable democratic aspirations, but it would be negligent not to examine their ability to achieve democracy in the turbulent environment created by the US invasion and against benchmarks of expectation that have been set not by me, but by the US and its Coalition. The same applies with the tribes – we need to explore in detail what the proponents of democracy are up against.

I suppose one way to get readers' attention is by an admitted opening cheap shot. But Anthony Bubalo buries an even cheaper one in the body of his critique – his suggestion that I confined my interviews to a "convenient sample" to make the story work. Wherever I go in Iraq, I make it my business to tap into the tribes, but the broader context in which I wrote was informed by interviews with perhaps a dozen Iraqi and regional experts and countless ordinary Iraqis. After reading Bubalo on *Mission Impossible*, it was difficult to know where to begin in response – because, despite his irritable tone, he agrees with or endorses much of what I wrote. It seems his principal objection is that I didn't write a different story.

Part II

So how might you find the post office in Baghdad? A good place to start is where worlds collide on the terrace at the Intercontinental Hotel on a balmy summer's night in Amman. A singer croons "New York, New York", but crashing through Sinatra's signature song is the thump of tribal drums from a wedding party deep inside the hotel. Guiding the waiters as they spread an Arab feast before us, Mudher al-Kharbit looks just like the multi-millionaire businessman that he is – from the swatch of silk in the breast-pocket of his well-cut suit, all the way down to shoes of fine crocodile skin. He crouches in his chair, smoking incessantly. And as he slows to find the right English words, he fills the pauses in frustrated Arabic: "Yanni? Yanni?" – "You know? You know?" But listen carefully – on this night, late in July, there is no talk of business. Al-Kharbit is speaking as the influential paramount sheikh of the two-million-strong Dulame tribe and head of the al-Kharbit clan, which dominate the tortured territories of western Iraq – Falluja and Ramadi and the endless deserts of al-Anbar province.

Al-Kharbit claims that he wants Iraq to have strong ties to US, but he is embittered by the fracturing of his immediate family's risky and covert relationship with the Americans. Readers of *Mission Impossible* may recall how, in the years before the war, the previous paramount sheikh of the Dulame and the younger half-brother of this man, Malik al-Kharbit, had been meeting secretly with US intelligence agents, briefing them on how to topple Saddam, pleading for help to mount a coup and even using their oil-services and construction business as a cover to ferry CIA agents into Iraq. But on 11 April, Sheikh Malik's palatial home was bombed by the US, apparently after a tip-off that Saddam Hussein was hiding there. Sheikh Malik and twenty-one members of the family died. In interviews soon after the April 2003 bombing, family members denied that Saddam was in the house. What seemed to have been a genuine love affair with America had been shattered because, in the doomsday language of the tribes, "Blood was spilled."

Over dinner in Amman, Mudher al-Kharbit reveals that one of the Americans' most-wanted "deck of cards" had in fact been in the house at the time of the attack. It was Rokan Abd al-Ghafur Suleiman, Saddam's personal bodyguard, who also oversaw the ousted dictator's relationships with the Iraqi tribes. Al-Kharbit is unapologetic: "He came for shelter and, according to Arab tradition, we could not refuse. But did they have to bomb? They could have surrounded the house and arrested him." Then, in an act of pure tribal one-upmanship, he recounts the fable of an ancient Arab warrior who killed his last horse so that he could feed his guests, before declaring: "History will remember that the al-Kharbits sacrificed twenty-two family members for the sake of our guest. It's the tribal way."

For now, al-Kharbit runs his Iraqi affairs by phone. He moves between the Intercontinental in Amman and his other home in Damascus, wary of returning to Iraq where another twenty-odd family members have been jailed as suspected insurgents. He is seized by tearful rage when he talks of a threat by a senior US officer to send the arrested al-Kharbit men to Guantanamo Bay and, after this, to start detaining the women of the clan. He spits his words: "If they start with the women, they will never see the end of it ... and we will never be quiet. I have told our people it's more honourable to shoot the women than to allow them to be taken prisoner." The Jordanian dining with us is deeply troubled by all of this. He urges: "The Americans should be trying to win the tribes over. Instead, they kill half of this man's family and they arrest the other half; and when he comes to talk to them, they demand that he take a polygraph test. If you don't know how to live in this part of the world, the Bedouin and the tribes will teach you a very expensive lesson. They don't care about the US election in November – they have been around for more than a thousand years, so they believe that time is on their side."

In a crisis like this, there is no bargain basement, so it's not surprising that al-Kharbit's expectations are huge. This is a man who is seriously bidding for control of the military and of national security in the new Iraq. His confidence is unnerving as he confirms much of what the experts cited in *Mission Impossible* said to me, but the sheikhs themselves would not be drawn on – Mudher al-Kharbit admits to having the power to end the insurgency, but he refuses to do so.

My first inclination is to dismiss him. But the Jordanian observer, a veteran analyst of Iraqi affairs who prefers not to be named, warns that this would be dangerous. And al-Kharbit underscores his point: "An Iraqi decision without the al-Kharbits is not a decision." And there are other indications: Iyad Allawi felt the need to see al-Kharbit when he came through Jordan on his first trip outside Iraq as its new prime minister; the sheikh produces a conciliatory letter from a US general pleading with him to return to Iraq to help end the violence; and there's an intriguing cast of American, British and Jordanian intelligence agents in the stories he tells. Al-Kharbit was instrumental in the release of up to a dozen of the foreign hostages held by insurgent groups in Iraq in July. And he enumerates the critical role played by his clan in every convulsion in Iraq's history, concluding: "[Before the coup] in 1968 the revolutionary army met in our house at Ramadi." Over several meetings his rhetoric escalates – except that in Amman and Baghdad I've been warned repeatedly that al-Kharbit does not engage in mere rhetoric. He means what he says, I'm told. When he is reminded that Allawi is building a 40,000-strong army, he laughs: "Ha! That's just a family brawl." And when the security crisis besetting Iraq comes up, he chuckles to another Iraqi in our company: "That's not resistance – we'll make Vietnam look like a picnic."

The average Washington neo-conservative will have as much difficulty accepting al-Kharbit's terms for peace as he will the sheikh's vision of a workable "democracy" in Iraq. But he demands that they test him: "Let them give me the most dangerous area of Iraq – al-Anbar province or Baghdad city – and I guarantee to make it quiet in twenty days or a month. If that works, I should be given control of the military and security services for all of Iraq." Al-Kharbit explains that he is not insisting on an immediate US withdrawal from the province: "They can patrol the towns, but they should remove their bases from the centres – and after a couple of months they would have to withdraw altogether. And I promise this: once they sign an agreement with me, there will be no foreign fighters in Iraq – all the strangers will be told to go. Their welcome will be over and no others will be able to cross our borders."

Then he proposes a new Iraq government of twin councils, one that would be made up of the born-to-rule, unelected tribal sheikhs and "other notables", which would have responsibility for defense and security; and another council of popularly elected representatives that would have carriage of the remaining business of government. It sounds like a variation of the Jordanian system or, as a Briton who joined us for dinner observed dryly, "He wants to replicate the House of Lords!" Al-Kharbit has put all of this to the Americans, claiming he told them: "Don't believe the reports now about me supporting the insurgents. But in one year's time I will be No. 1 in the resistance." It's an unambiguous threat.

The band changes gear. They sing "Hotel California" as al-Kharbit announces that he has bought a ticket to Washington. He'll have nothing to do with the US troops in Iraq and he dismisses Prime Minister Allawi and his interim government as "burnt", but he wants to put his case directly to the Pentagon and the State Department. So far, however, there has been little headway in back-channel attempts to arrange for him to talk directly to Washington.

The day after dinner at the Intercontinental, I call Washington to test what I'm being told about the power of al-Kharbit and the Dulame tribe. I track down Amatzia Baram, an Iraq specialist at the University of Haifa and the Washington-based US Institute of Peace. Baram worries that US forces are overplaying their hand with al-Kharbit. He proffers that the sheikh is overstating his power, but not by much: "His family were trusted go-betweens on the most sensitive issues for Saddam Hussein and the late King Hussein of Jordan. He can't stop all the resistance in Iraq, but in al-Anbar, and especially in Ramadi, he is very important. I have no doubt that he could reduce the resistance by as much as 85 per cent in Ramadi and maybe 35 per cent in other areas. In Falluja the response would depend on what he had to offer in return for peace. The only problem is that I don't know if the US understands how useful he would be – if he could be bought off."

Before al-Kharbit could pursue his Washington mission all hell broke loose in Ramadi, his hometown. The tribal sheikhs and US commanders in the city are at odds over just what sparked the late July eruption. Al-Kharbit says the fuse was lit by an American decision to force his 77-year-old uncle and fellow sheikh, Abdul Razak al-Kharbit, into exile. The US says "nonsense" and describes the Wednesday on which the fighting started as just another bloody-minded day for insurgents who ambushed a US supply convoy as it motored through Ramadi.

The Americans can't go on as they are. Only days before the Ramadi eruption, the US officers in al-Anbar spoke of pulling back to base – they were sick of being shot at by insurgents who simply refuse to bow to US force. But they hoped too that the new Iraqi government and its security forces would fill the power vacuum. Not so – yet. The city went mad as news spread of the red-faced old man's departure to Jordan, for whatever reasons and on whoever's orders. In an email exchange, a military spokesman denied to me that a sheikh had been exiled, but days later a UPI reporter embedded with the US military in Ramadi quoted a senior intelligence officer to the effect that a high-profile member of the local community had been forced to choose between imprisonment in Abu Ghraib or exile in Qatar.

Businesses in Ramadi were quickly shuttered as the thunder of rocket-propelled grenades, mortars, bombs and machine-gun fire ripped through its streets and alleyways. The locals rigged deadly car and roadside bombs and threw up pre-planned ambushes; the Americans called in air-support and hundreds of US Marines poured in for what became a four-hour opening street battle. More than twenty-five people died and dozens more were injured or arrested.

As the sun set and the dust settled, US surveillance helicopters were thick in the air as small funeral processions made their way to local cemeteries. The US denied a local claim that one of its helicopters had been brought down, and the spokesman offered this emailed explanation of the detention of the al-Kharbit men: "Approximately 20 [people] were detained earlier this month, but only a small number of them are thought to be actual members of the al-Kharbit family. Four of the detainees were sent to Abu Ghraib for involvement in facilitating cross-border movement of insurgents, financing insurgent activity and threats to kill the Governor." The clash didn't let up, though. A week later, the insurgents launched a series of co-ordinated raids on US posts in and around the city, killing two Americans and wounding eleven more, and damaging two US aircraft. And a couple of days after the departure of the old man there was payback for his expulsion – in a brazen daylight attack the three teenage and older sons of the US-appointed provincial governor, Abdul Karim Burghis al-Rawi, were kidnapped and their home was torched, prompting al-Kharbit to opine: "It was a clean attack – they didn't touch the women in the house."

The closest the US has come to apologising for the death of twenty-two members of the al-Kharbit family in the sixteen months since the US occupation began is a carefully worded, unsigned letter in the name of Major General J.M. Mattis, of the First Marine Division, in Ramadi. A copy was delivered to al-Kharbit in Amman. It reads, in part: "There has been trouble between the Kharbit family and the Americans in the past, but men of vision look to the future and put the past behind them. We have both mourned our losses, and better understand each other's points of view. We are using this opportunity to extend the hand of friendship to you and to your tribe. As a gesture of this friendship, we invite you to return to al-Anbar province to live in peace ... the Kharbits are an old tribe that has much influence over lesser tribes. We require [your] help in controlling these tribes and teaching them a life of truth and peace, instead of crime and violence."

Al-Kharbit is impressed by the sentiment – he even describes Mattis as "a very nice man". But he believes the general is in the thrall of the CIA and other intelligence agencies that are being fooled by what he calls "the rubbish guys" of al-Anbar – he names a reputed former Saddam bagman, who some say has now embarked on a new business career with millions he was holding for the ousted Iraqi leader, and an enemy Ramadi sheikh as being among those he says are attempting to manipulate events in al-Anbar and to do his family down. But chief among his "rubbish guys" is Iraq's interim Prime Minister, Iyad Allawi. After their inconclusive meeting in Amman, al-Kharbit remains leery: "Allawi's real motive is to show the US that the man they think is driving everyone crazy is in his pocket. But if the Americans didn't understand the power and standing of my family, Allawi has just shown it to them by his need to meet me."

Notwithstanding the need that Allawi felt to talk to him; the endorsements in Baghdad, Amman and Washington; the sentiment of the Mattis letter; and the fact that after the Ramadi violence, a three-man delegation from the US embassy in Baghdad traipsed all the way to Amman to talk to al-Kharbit, the US intelligence team in Ramadi seems to have gone into psy-ops overdrive in a effort to discredit the man who once was one of their staunchest allies. They found a receptive ear in an embedded reporter from United Press International, who quoted an unnamed Marine intelligence officer claiming that al-Kharbit had become an unbalanced megalomaniac as a result of physical abuse and neglect he suffered as the child of a sheikh who had two intensively competitive wives. Al-Kharbit, according to UPI, had won the role of sheikh by foul means; had become a "cash cow for the insurgency" on the back of a lucrative smuggling empire; and had been far too cosy with Saddam's regime. The intelligence officer was quoted: "He was a businessman, a thug with money, well dressed, and he sucked up to Saddam. Really. I've talked to his family. At least four [of them] diagnose him as mentally disturbed, one of them a doctor. We have independent assessments of his writings, some intercepts. He's a megalomaniac. It's a [medical] diagnosis. He has delusions of grandeur."

I had a translator read the UPI report to Mudher in Arabic. He laughed off most of it and when she reached the "megalomaniac" comment, he scratched his nose and said: "That's good, isn't it?" But for the most part, he batted back each of the allegations and lectured the Americans on the shabbiness of their intelligence work: "They get it from cheap guys. It's not very professional – don't they know how to go step by step?"

Almost 500,000 people live in the dust-bowl towns of al-Anbar. Apart from Ramadi, its other main city is Falluja, the scene of the bloody battle, in which as many as 800 died, between US forces and the insurgency in April 2004. The Americans have lost more than 120 men in the province since President George W. Bush declared an end to major combat in May 2003 – fifteen of them since the 28 June handover of power. Such is the resistance, the Americans have declared much of Ramadi and nearby towns to be no-go areas, and they say they have narrowed their objective in the city to protecting a key local supply line – the highway through the town. An American reporter embedded with US troops near Ramadi quoted Major Thomas Neemeyer, head of intelligence for the 1st Brigade of the 1st Infantry Division: "They cannot militarily overwhelm us, but we cannot deliver a knockout blow, either," he said. "It creates a form of stalemate." Neemeyer told the Knight Ridder reporter: "There's a possibility that we'll say we'll protect the government and keep travel routes open, and for the rest of them, to hell with 'em. To a certain degree we've already done it; we've reduced our presence."

Al-Kharbit says he is working the scratchy phone lines to Ramadi every night till 3 a.m., trying to quell the violence. "What's happening now is bad for us. It would have been ten times worse than Falluja if I didn't settle them down – everyone lost their temper; and now there is too much tension," he says.

It all sounds very menacing. Al-Kharbit's "I told you so" speeches are read here in Jordan as self-absolution ahead of what might happen in al-Anbar if he does not get his way. He told me: "All that I told the US before the war has been proved right, so this will be my last advice. If the US will not listen, I will go home; do nothing; and when the place explodes, they will accuse me of starting it. They wanted me on the Iraqi Governing Council. I wouldn't do it unless it was by election; they offered me money and business deals – I said 'No.' So let them leave us alone. I know that, as the days go by, the people they rely on now will fall and they will come back to me, and I will refuse to help them." And he concluded not so cryptically: "After that, I will do what I'm going to do."

In Amman, it is easier – and perhaps more frightening – than in Baghdad to see how the Ramadi convulsions feed into regional power-plays. Al-Kharbit wants to talk to the Americans but Washington is giving him the cold shoulder. The Turks, wary of Kurdish autonomy in northern Iraq, are putting out feelers to him, while Baghdad has unsubtly threatened to send proven Kurdish fighters to sort out predominantly Sunni al-Anbar. But the greatest anxiety here is about the role of Syria and Iran. These regimes are very close – both are under US sanctions and are vehemently anti-American, and the prospect of a US-dominated Iraq sandwiched between them is a cause of deep anxiety. Al-Kharbit is letting it be known that if he has nowhere else to turn, he does have a direct line to Damascus – recently he has had three meetings with the Syrian President, Bashar Asad. The Jordanian analyst, who prefers not to be named, says: "He needs to survive. He will go to whoever supports him."

Watching events unfold from his study in Washington, Baram argues that Washington cannot deliver on al-Kharbit's outlandish demands, but that the US needs some of what al-Kharbit is offering. So, he concludes, "Middle East negotiations must take place." Amidst so much Iraqi gloom, Baram sees positive signs: "Al-Kharbit can do some of what he says he will do – so they should test him; and after the Americans killed so many of his family, it's not easy for him to swallow his pride and offer to talk to Washington. It means he thinks that being arm's length from the US is not a good idea and that this is the thinking of the people around him. He is saying that he has demonstrated his nuisance value, and now he wants to cash in."

Between tales of carousing on the trans-Atlantic Concorde and dining with his Jewish friends in Montreal, al-Kharbit also reveals that he is feeling the heat from his tribe. "We don't have anyone to save our family and our country," he told me, complaining of a stream of phone calls from people in Ramadi demanding to know why he is still in Jordan. An observer said: "He feels that he is losing his grip on the tribe. He has to go back to them with one of two things. Either the US is listening to him – or it's not, in which case the response in al-Anbar will be: 'Let's give them hell.' And that'll make Falluja look like a tickle. The absurdity of all this is that the Americans were talking about the Sunni Triangle before the war. Al-Kharbit and his tribe were the only people who didn't fire a shot at the Americans and they allowed US Special Forces into the country three months before the war started."

Paul McGeough

Les Murray

The Ball Owns Me

for Germaine Greer with kind regards

My great grand-uncle invented haute couture. Tiens,
I am related to Je Reviens!

It is the line of Worth, Grandmother's family
that excuses me from chic. It's been done for me.

When Worths from Coolongolook, both Koori and white,
came out of Fromelles trenches on leave from the fight

they went up to Paris and daringly located
the House of Worth. At the doors, they hesitated –

but were swept from inquiry to welcome to magnificence:
You have come around the world to rescue France,

dear cousins. Nothing is too good for you!
Feast now and every visit. Make us your rendezvous.

I checked this with Worths, the senior ones still living:
Didn't you know that? they said. *Don't you know anything?*

Les Murray

Anthony Bubalo has served in Australia's embassies in Saudi Arabia and in Israel. More recently he was the senior speechwriter of the Department of Foreign Affairs and Trade, and a director on its Iraq Task Force. He also served as Middle East Analyst in the Office of National Assessments from 1996 to 1998. He is currently a Research Fellow at the Lowy Institute for International Policy.

Inga Clendinnen is the author of *Ambivalent Conquests: Spaniard and Maya in Yucatan 1517–1577*, *Aztecs: An Interpretation*, *Reading the Holocaust*, *Tiger's Eye* and, most recently, *Dancing with Strangers*, which won the 2004 Kiriyama Prize for Non-Fiction.

Paul McGeough is a former editor of the *Sydney Morning Herald*. He has been a reporter for almost thirty years, covering international conflict since the 1990–91 Gulf War. McGeough's work has earned Australia's highest journalistic honours, including the 2003 Walkley Award for his coverage of the Iraq War.

Les Murray's latest book in Australia is *Learning Human: New Selected Poems* (Duffy & Snellgrove, 2003).

Margaret Simons' book *The Meeting of the Waters: The Hindmarsh Island Affair* won the Queensland Premier's Literary Award for Non-Fiction in 2003 and was short-listed for numerous other awards. Her book of reportage about the operations of the Canberra press gallery, *Fit to Print*, was published in 1999. Between 1987 and 1989, she covered the Fitzgerald Inquiry in Queensland for the *Age* and the *Sydney Morning Herald*, before being seconded to Fitzgerald's staff as a consultant to assist in the writing of his final report. Her most recent book is *Resurrection in a Bucket*.

www.ingramcontent.com/pod-product-compliance
Lightning Source LLC
Chambersburg PA
CBHW081400270326
41930CB00015B/3365